Brad

Thank you for your service
in the Navy. Hope you
enjoy the book.

Steve Burchik

16 FEB 2016

# COMPASS
# AND A CAMERA
# A YEAR IN
# VIETNAM

By Steven

www.stevenburchik.com

Sharlin-K Press
San Ramon, CA

ISBN-10: 0692276297
ISBN-13: 978-0692276297

# ACKNOWLEDGMENTS

I would like to thank the following people for their inspiration, support and assistance.

The members of D Company, Second Battalion, 18th Infantry Regiment, my brothers in arms who helped me learn the skills needed to survive. Your vigilance and mutual support allowed me to be one of the lucky ones who returned and lived long enough to write this book. Thank you for having my back. My lifelong brothers, Bruce and Gary, who encouraged me to explore new boundaries and were always there with a word of support or some practical advice at just the right time. The brothers and faculty at Manhattan College who provided the opportunity to develop my love of writing at one of the few institutions with two college newspapers. The editors at the *New York Daily News*-on the night shift, who encouraged my career aspirations while I was working there as an undergraduate. My children, the cheering squad who patiently sat through many family slide presentations and thought that this book would be a good project for me.

Arlene Addison who said, yes, young people do want to hear about the experiences of Vietnam. Alan Weller, who was honestly interested in the Vietnam combat experience and was excited about seeing my slides and photographs. He encouraged me to prepare a presentation for a group in Berkeley. When I expressed some reservations about the project, he said, "It's been forty years. There are many people who want to hear from the individuals who fought there." Phil Gibbons, a writer and film director, who made a number of suggestions when I started the outline of the book and then reviewed the manuscript and offered specifics to improve the flow and readability. Kim Nguyen, who assisted me with the Vietnamese translations.

Finally, I must acknowledge Christina, who was a constant source of support and encouragement during my tour in Vietnam and in all the years since. She thoughtfully saved each of the daily letters that I sent her. Those letters, combined with the photos, provided a detailed contemporaneous account of my experience, which enabled this project to come to life. She is also an excellent writer and made numerous suggestions to improve the book by emphasizing the most interesting episodes and prudently editing many of the necessary but tedious details of life in the boonies.

# IN MEMORIAM

Private First Class Willie Gene Cooper

Specialist Fourth Class Frederick Eugene Rouse

Private First Class Richard Saenz

Private First Class Ray Gene Wilson

and

Sergeant Robert John Ollikainen

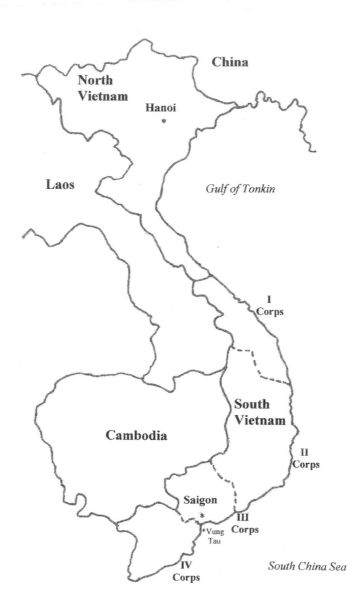

Map  -  Vietnam 1968

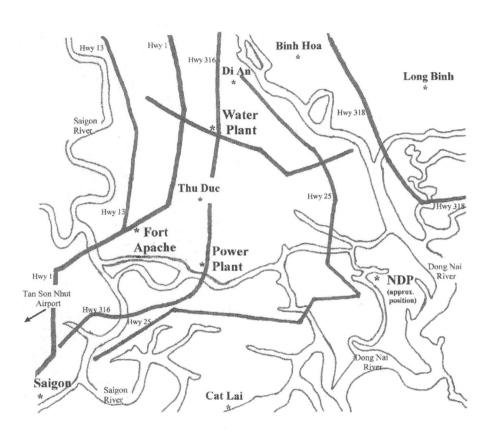

Map - Area of Operation 2nd Bn 18th Infantry 1968

# TIMELINE OF LOCATIONS

<u>1968</u>

| | |
|---|---|
| Arrive in Long Binh | Jun 28 |
| Move to Di An | Jul 3 |
| Move to Water Plant | Jul 12 |
| Move to NDP | Sep 12 |
| Move to Fort Apache | Nov 26 |

<u>1969</u>

| | |
|---|---|
| R&R - Australia | Jan 26 |
| Move to Di An | Mar 7 |
| Move to Fort Pawnee | Mar 11 |
| Move to Di An | Mar 19 |
| Move to Fort Apache | Apr 2 |
| Move to Power Plant | Apr 19 |
| R&R - Vung Tau | May 26 |
| Move to Di An | May 31 |
| Fly to States | Jun 10 |

# CONTENTS

# CHAPTER 1

# ARRIVING "IN-COUNTRY"

My army career began with infantry training in various military bases on the East Coast. In the late spring of 1968, I received my orders to report for duty in Vietnam. Before starting that life-changing journey, I spent a week on leave in New York City with family, friends, and my fiancée, Christina.

I had enlisted in the army with mixed feelings about the service. I was not particularly eager to experience combat, although that was highly likely in the late sixties. My student deferment had expired when I graduated from college. This meant that I was subject to the draft and could be called to report for military service at any time, in a month, six months, or later. This also meant that plans for starting a career would be tenuous at best, since I still faced the prospect of having to leave a new job shortly after going through the time and effort of finding one. The lottery system for the draft would not be implemented until December 1969.

There were also personal feelings that were factors in the decision. Both sides of my family had Slavic backgrounds. My father's family had come from Czechoslovakia, and my mother's family was from Poland. I had grown up with a deep awareness that these countries were trapped behind the Iron Curtain under the communist system. I had gone to grammar school with some children whose families had escaped from Hungary after the ill-fated uprising in 1956. I felt some personal obligation to help prevent the further spread of communism, and Vietnam looked like the place where the United States was taking a stand.

I left New York on June 24, 1968, and arrived in San Francisco before heading to the nearby Oakland Army Base. It was my first visit to the City by the Bay, and I was determined to thoroughly enjoy the sights and sounds of San Francisco on my last privileged day of independence. I crisscrossed the city from the Golden Gate Bridge to Chinatown, ending up at Fisherman's Wharf. At the time I thought that it was an amazing city and that the people who lived there were indeed fortunate. Since I was focused on the near-term challenges I was about to face, I never considered the possibility that I might one day live or work near this idyllic place.

The next day I reported to Oakland Army Base, my final contact with the United States before heading overseas. Processing—consisting of picking up new clothing and partial pay and receiving a final cholera shot—took a day and a half.

At 7:00 p.m. on Wednesday I found myself sitting on a bunk in a large warehouse-type building on Oakland Army Base serving as a ready room for overseas shipments. My bunk was one of about two thousand bunks in this section of the building, and I estimated that the entire structure had about ten thousand bunks! We were scheduled to leave at 3:50 a.m. Thursday and travel by bus to Travis Air Force Base.

From there we'd travel to Vietnam in a Braniff Boeing 707, a trip of eighteen hours including the refueling stops. I had come to California on the friendly skies of United, but I'd be leaving for the not-so-friendly skies of Braniff.

Morale was pretty high, although there was a certain amount of apprehension, especially in the toned-down nature of the jokes at which everyone laughed only halfheartedly. There was also a definite lack of horseplay. I remained pretty calm and curious to see what Vietnam would be like.

We woke early on Thursday morning and, in the dark, boarded the bus for the ride to Travis Air Force Base. The bus stopped at the flight line and, dressed in Class A khaki short-sleeve summer uniforms, we boarded the pale-green Braniff 707 jet that would fly us to Vietnam.

The whole trip had a sense of incongruity. Here were a couple hundred GIs on our way to war in a beautiful pale-green jet with a crisp blue-and-white interior. As one soldier asked out loud, "Is this trip really necessary?" Four pretty flight attendants continually served delicious meals. Every few hours they changed into a different stylish outfit designed by Gucci or some other famous designer. It sure beat the accounts that I'd read about World War II, when soldiers were seasick for two or three weeks while they made the trip on some cattle boat or steamer.

The pale-green jet took off at 6:00 a.m. and landed about six hours later at 7:30 a.m. in Honolulu for a refueling stop. We spent an hour in the airport terminal watching swans in the garden pond, palm trees, and blue-and-white-striped jeep tourist taxis. When the refueling was completed we continued our flight across the Pacific. As we took off, I caught a glimpse of Diamond Head and thought of the military history of this spot, where another war in the Pacific had started twenty-seven years earlier.

It was now early afternoon on Friday, since we had crossed the International Date Line. We made another refueling stop at Clark Air Force Base in the Philippines. The airfield was large and impressive. There were dozens of planes on the field, including huge air force cargo planes. The land around the airfield was relatively flat, but beyond the base, we could see the impressive outline of Mount Pinatubo. Years later, Mount Pinatubo would erupt and cover the land occupied by this airfield with a heavy coating of volcanic ash. The green jet took off again on its final leg, a two-and-a-half-hour flight to Vietnam.

As we approached the coast of Vietnam, the plane grew silent. I looked around the cabin and wondered how many of us would be on a similar plane a year from now returning home. Each man was probably thinking the same thoughts. We had all seen the daily reports in newspapers and on TV and radio about the numbers of soldiers killed and in our rational minds understood that there would be some empty seats. But our hopeful optimism convinced us that our odds were pretty favorable; we had a good chance of making it if we followed the lessons from our training and didn't take unnecessary risks. I realized I might be killed, but I assumed that it would most likely be the "other guy." Perhaps this was selfish, but this thought allowed me to function for the next twelve months.

The stewardesses who had been friendly and chatty on most of the trip became quiet and reserved. They also understood that the human cargo they were helping deliver to the war zone would inevitably result in losses to some families back in the States.

It was late afternoon in Vietnam as we made the final approach to the airfield at Bien Hoa. It had been raining, so we flew through low clouds. We began to see the small rooftops of homes in a village near the landing site. Everything looked brown and gray. We finally touched down at 4:00 p.m. on Friday, June 28, picked up our duffel bags, and boarded buses for the ride to the large base at Long Binh. The buses were the same large olive-drab-colored buses used in training at bases all over the United States. We immediately noticed one key difference. All of the windows had a hard metal mesh covering. The driver explained that the road we were taking was relatively safe, but there had been incidents in the past when grenades were thrown into the bus.

Then we noticed the smell of the country, a moist, damp smell, probably a combination of rotting trash, decaying leaves, and other vegetation. The intensity varied as we drove along, stronger near the small villages and hamlets and milder in the open areas. We soon learned that most villages did not have sewer systems or trash collection systems. People used canals and riverbanks as latrines and burned their trash.

When we arrived in Long Binh we were assigned to a replacement barracks. I was impressed by its immense size and the neatly stacked sandbags surrounding every building and barracks. The sandbags were to protect the occupants from mortar and rocket fire. We had definitely arrived in Vietnam.

There was also some humor in this new situation. We passed a service club where you could buy a drink if you were lucky enough to have some free time (we didn't). The name of the club was "Jet Set Service Club." Jet Set was a sixties term for the rich and famous who flew internationally to attend parties and social gatherings. We had arrived by jet, but this was definitely not a party.

Since we were the new "grunts" in-country, our duties were pretty basic. We spent three days on KP, guard duty, and filling sandbags. The basic objective was to keep us busy while acclimating to the new time zone and environment.

Monday, July 1, we moved by truck to Di An, headquarters for the 1st Infantry Division, also known as the Big Red One, the oldest and one of the most famous divisions in army history.[1]

The 1st Infantry Division arrived in Vietnam on July 12, 1965, landing at Cam Rahn Bay. Major battles prior to my arrival included

---

1 It has seen continuous service since first being formed on May 24, 1917, with the name First Expeditionary Division, later designated as the 1st Infantry Division. The first units sailed to Europe from New York on June 14, 1917, and proceeded to Le Havre, France, to fight in World War I. Major campaigns included Catigny, Lorraine, Saint Michael, and Muse-Argonne. Five Medals of Honor were awarded during this conflict.

After World War I, it was demobilized, and the headquarters was moved to Fort Hamilton in Brooklyn, New York. The headquarters was later moved several times: to Fort Benning, Georgia, on November 19, 1939; Sabine Parish, Louisiana, on May 11, 1940; Fort Hamilton, New York, on June 5, 1940; Fort Devens, Massachusetts, on February 4, 1941, and Indiantown Gap Military Reservation, Pennsylvania, on June 21, 1942. In 1955, the Big Red One moved to its most recent home at Fort Riley, Kansas.

During World War II, the division departed New York on August 1, 1942, for a stop in England before participating in the Allied invasion of French North Africa. The unit also participated in the invasion of Sicily, D-Day at Omaha Beach, as well as battles at Saint-Lo, Aachen, the Battle of the Bulge in the Ardennes, Remagen, and the Ruhr Pocket. Sixteen Medals of Honor were awarded during this war.

Bushmaster I and II, Operation Crimp, Operation Attleboro, Operation Cedar Falls, Operation Junction City, and the Tet Offensive of 1968 to secure Tan Son Nhut Air Base. A total of 6,146 members would be killed, and 16,019 would be wounded during the entire Vietnam conflict. The division members would receive eleven Medals of Honor during this war.

Wednesday, July 3, I was assigned to my permanent unit: D Company, Second Battalion, 18th Infantry Brigade, 1st Infantry Division. We were sometimes referred to as the Second of the 18th. The unit was also known as the 18th Infantry Regiment which was first formed in 1861. My rank was Specialist 4th Class (Spec 4), my MOS (military occupation specialty) was 11B20, and I was part of the weapons platoon that supported three other infantry platoons. Our platoon's armament included three M-29, mortars—81 mm, two M-60 machine guns, a couple of M-79 grenade launchers, and individual M-16 assault rifles for the rest of the platoon.

A mortar is a long metal tube that works like a small artillery piece. It fires a variety of different shells that have a range of about forty-five hundred meters.

There were about twenty-five men in our platoon. There are four platoons in a company and five companies in a battalion. The other guys in the platoon weren't as young as those in basic training or AIT. The average age here was about twenty or twenty-one, with several who were twenty-three and twenty-four years old. I was twenty-three. These were my comrades and brothers for the next twelve months. I hoped that I would be able to live up to their expectations and mine. Our survival would depend on mutual trust and support for each other.

Everyone seemed very serious and tense, even when playing cards or hanging out in the barracks. There was an edge to the mood, and I couldn't figure it out. When I asked a couple of the guys who had been in the platoon for some time, I learned that one of the soldiers in the company had been killed in combat five days earlier as a result of multiple fragmentation wounds. I realized he died on the same day I arrived in Vietnam.

The Di An camp was a large facility, not as big as Long Binh, but still impressive. It was four miles long and one mile wide, surrounded by concertina wire (large coils of barbed wire), enclosing an airport, heliport, electric generator, paved roads, an ice plant, and a couple of tank companies. Every base in Vietnam had a sign with little boards painted in different colors to indicate the condition of military situations at any given time. The colors were white, yellow, and red. A white alert meant there was a potential conflict, but nothing immediate. The yellow alert meant that an attack was imminent. The red alert showed that we were currently under attack.

The primary missions of the 1st Infantry Division were to keep Highway 13 open and to protect and defend Saigon. Highway 13 (also known as "Thunder Road") starts in the town of Thu Duc northeast of Saigon and runs north to Cambodia. This was the Division's AO (area of operation).

A barracks consisting of a long narrow wood-frame building sitting on a concrete slab was to be my home for the next two weeks. The interior was bare except for a row of metal cots along each of the long walls and a wooden footlocker in front of each cot. Assorted packs and gear hung from a nail above each cot. Once again, I was assigned to tasks that included filling sandbags and pulling guard duty.

Although we heard our artillery pieces at night as they shelled suspected enemy positions, I hadn't yet seen any fighting.

Nights were spent on guard duty with two other men inside a sandbagged bunker about one hundred feet from the perimeter wire. We had two M-16s, a grenade launcher, several claymore mines, six hand grenades, and several hundred rounds of ammunition. We took turns on watch, so that we were able to sleep part of the time.

I was also assigned to the morning garbage detail, picking up the garbage from our company area and driving it to a burning pit at the edge of the camp. We would no sooner park the truck when fifteen Vietnamese kids would eagerly jump in and start going through the garbage looking for gum, C-rations, empty sandbags, and anything else that was salvageable.

On Thursday, July 4, we were treated to a special meal in the evening. The cooks set up a large grill outside the mess area and grilled steaks for everyone. There was also a small cart filled with beer cans and blocks of ice. This was an exceptional treat to celebrate the Fourth of July. Everyone enjoyed a beer or two and a good meal. There was no excessive drinking because we knew we might be called to defend the base, even though we felt relatively safe here. After dark there was an impromptu fireworks show consisting of signal flares: red, white, and green star clusters accompanied by the standard red and white parachute flares. Several people fired hand flares into the night sky. The red and white flares headed upward and drifted slowly back to earth on small parachutes. Not quite like the fireworks show at the county fair, but close enough to remind us of celebrations back home.

We never had a firm schedule for events in Vietnam. The army operated on a system of "hurry up and wait." We would rush to get on a truck or go to a point on a map and wait for the next order. The orders could be changed or reversed at any time, so it helped to have a flexible mental attitude that recognized constant change as a way of life. I had been assigned to the brigade replacement school. My squad leader told me that I would probably start out as a radio operator after I finished the training at the school. Since the radio weighed about twenty-five pounds, I was not particularly thrilled about the job, but I didn't have much choice in the matter.

On Saturday, July 6, I started a seven-day course on in-country techniques for fighting and survival. The official name was the 2nd Brigade Replacement Training School. The informal name was Dagger University which was painted on the metal wall behind a small metal grandstand used by our instructors. We had all been through the standard infantry training programs in the States which included marksmanship, low crawling under machine gun fire, handling exposure to CS gas (tear gas), first aid, and infantry tactics. The new in-country course covered just about everything we needed to know to avoid danger and fatal mistakes. We covered mines, booby traps, smoke bombs, and signal flares.

Author, (with the Spec 4 patch) boards the Vietnam-bound plane after a refueling stop in Honolulu.

Welcome sign for D 2nd of the 18th.

A Fourth of July treat, steaks and beer after only six days in-country.

Outdoor training was an important part of our day. One day we went through a trail marked DEATH WALK, DO NOT ENTER WITHOUT GUIDE. It included a variety of booby traps, including trip wires attached to simulated grenades and punji pits (sharpened stakes in a hole in the ground covered with leaves or grass). Another area had signs in Vietnamese (for the civilians) that read: "Nguy hiem cam vuot qua" (Do not pass here) and "Bat tuan se bi ban" (You will be shot if you disobey). It was a sobering introduction to the dangers we might face.

We also got training on disassembling and cleaning the M-16 rifle. Most of us had practiced with the larger and heavier M-14 in stateside training. However, the M-16 was to be our primary weapon in Vietnam.

Since helicopters were a major mode of transportation, we spent a good deal of time practicing getting on and off, with an emphasis on speed. One of the most risky times in the field is when entering or leaving the chopper, because it is on or close to the ground and at the highest risk for receiving enemy fire. The practice chopper was a bare shell with no front window and no blades on top or at the back. Two wooden boards replaced the seats. The paint was chipped and cracked. The chopper had no doors. The instructor explained when helicopters were first introduced to the Vietnam

COMPASS AND A CAMERA

conflict, they found that doors slowed entry and exit time, so they were removed or left open when flying on real missions.

The army had not paid a contractor for a simulator. We were practicing on a real helicopter that had flown on real missions. We wondered what happened to the pilots and crew that led to the current duty station for this bird.

At the end of training each day, we returned to our barracks. The food was pretty good. We got a fresh glass of milk every morning which was brought in from a Foremost plant in Saigon. We also got ice cream for dessert every three or four days. There were enlisted men's clubs on the base that sold cold beer and soda. Most food cooling was done with large blocks of ice from the base ice plant.

Not surprisingly, during training I wasn't getting much sleep, because I was working twenty-four hours a day. We attended classes from 07:30 to 17:30 in the evening.[2] Then guard duty from 18:30 at night until 06:30 the next morning, although we took turns sleeping, so one person was always awake at any given time. We had an hour in the morning and again in the evening to eat, change clothes, and get gear ready for class or guard duty. To complicate things, the malaria pills had some nasty side effects, including vomiting and diarrhea, so I was very uncomfortable during training. The side effects eventually wore off after a few days.

The type of work that my regular unit did depended on whether or not they were at a remote base camp. Right now, they had been in Di An since June 5, but just prior to that they were in the field for three months. There was no telling how much longer my company would be here. While I was in replacement training, they worked

---

2  Military time is used in my descriptions. It's based on a twenty-four-hour clock and is designed to avoid confusion with important events, such as firing artillery at 7:00 (a.m. or p.m.?). It starts at 00:00 for midnight and continues normally until 12:00, which is noon. Then you add twelve hours to every time in the second half of the day, so that 1:30 p.m. is added to 12:00, resulting in 13:30 hours. We usually skip the word "hours" after the numerical time, because it is implied.

at night. Each evening at about 18:30, they boarded trucks or helicopters and were dropped off at some point a few miles from camp. They marched for about an hour and then set up an ambush along a river, trail, etc. They'd sit in the ambush position until daybreak then return to camp to get some sleep. When based in the field, they'd dig in and set up a patrol base that might last from several days to several months. The mortar platoon (my platoon) stayed in the base and operated the mortars while the other three infantry platoons went out on patrols. We'd also go out in the field when more troops were needed for a mission.

Radios were being played constantly in the barracks day and night. There were five or six stations that broadcast American music and programs. Some of the more popular songs we'd hear were "Hey, Jude," "We Gotta Get Out of This Place," "Sittin' on the Dock of the Bay," and "Born to be Wild." I also remember hearing a *Meet the Press* interview with Eugene McCarthy. Most of the clubs on the base had TV sets that played shows from AFVN (Armed Forces Vietnam Network), but I had no time to watch.

On Friday, July 12, I completed the Dagger University course. We set up a practice daylight ambush in a pretty secure area. We didn't expect any contact, and there was none. On the way back, we were walking through tall grass when I looked to the left and saw a cobra with its hooded head raised two feet from me. I could have reached out and patted its head. I just kept walking past it. This experience remained with me as a frightening and memorable moment. We headed back to the barracks.

When we reached the barracks, everything was in turmoil. The company was leaving Di An. We packed up all of our gear, boarded a truck, and moved to my first live base camp in Vietnam. It was the water filtration plant located a few miles north of Saigon that supplied all of the water for Saigon. One of our missions would be to guard this location.

# CHAPTER 2

# WATER PLANT—FIRST MISSIONS

The water plant had a unique layout. A major landmark was the large cement water tower, that climbed more than a hundred feet in the air. The pipes inside maintained the water pressure needed to transport the water to Saigon. There were openings at the top, so that the tower could also be used as an observation post to protect the water plant. Within the compound, there were several large filtration ponds that looked like oversize swimming pools. Highway 316, a busy transportation route, passed in front of the plant. This was to be my home for the next two months.

We were located next to the main building and lived in tents. The "tents" were not really tents, but rather makeshift shelters comprised of a couple of long metal engineer stakes laid over four- or five-foot-tall sandbag walls. The stakes were then covered with dark-green plastic ponchos that were tied together to keep out the rain. The door was a flexible opening on one side made with clear plastic sheets. We affectionately called the dwelling our "hootch." There was usually room for two or three soldiers. Each man had a metal-frame cot covered with stiff canvas. The cot had a lightweight camouflage-color poncho liner that could be used as a mattress or light blanket, depending on the temperature. Gear was stored under the cots or at the far end of the hootch.

Most had dirt floors, but a few had rough wooden floors. The residents were quite resourceful. Since we were a mortar platoon, we had a constant supply of wooden ammo boxes for the mortars that also included large clear sheets of thick plastic. We also used the empty ammo boxes to build walls for the hootches by filling them with dirt. They formed a straighter wall than sandbags and provided just as much protection from incoming fire from mortars, rockets, and bullets.

The rainy monsoon season had started, and the ground was muddy much of the time. There was a network of streets, the width of sidewalks, (made from empty ammo boxes) leading from each hootch to a central avenue and then to the various mortar pits. Each of the streets and the main avenue had names, including Shower Lane, Moore Ave. (named after the platoon sergeant), FDC Alley (fire direction center), DEROS Street (date of expected return from overseas) and Dead End Street.

Critical class at Dagger University: we broke down and cleaned the M-16 rifle. For most of us, it was the first time we had used this weapon, since we trained with the older M-14 in stateside bases.

Empty ammo boxes served as walkways on the way to our "hootches" at the water plant. In heavy rains, the ground became a sea of mud.

The water tower maintained water pressure for
Saigon and served as a lookout point.

The experienced soldiers in the platoon were happy that we moved to this base of operations. In addition to the hot breakfast in the morning and the hot dinner at night, there were showers available due to the ample supply of fresh water.

Our infantry company shared this facility with a tank unit from the 11th Armored Cavalry. They had several tanks here, and their crews were constantly performing maintenance on the tanks when they were not in use on the main roads. Most of the surrounding terrain was soft ground covered with mud or water, limiting the mobility of tanks. It was a provocative sight to see the spare tank treads coiled up in a tight roll standing five or six feet tall. In front of the water plant facing the highway, there was a large grassy open area used as a helicopter landing strip to fly us out on missions. It was enclosed by a tall fence to prevent anyone from entering from the road.

We also shared this base with an artillery unit on the opposite side of the water plant. They exhibited esprit de corps by painting names on the guns such as Fanny Hill, etc. and took great pains to keep their 105 mm howitzers clean and polished between firing missions.

My first full day at the water plant was spent helping to dig a mortar pit and filling sandbags to protect the mortar crew. The pit was a hole in the ground eleven feet in diameter and three feet deep.

On Sunday, July 14, we quickly finished breakfast, grabbed our gear and headed to the grassy plot at the edge of the water plant. We were headed out on our first live combat mission. About fifteen minutes later five choppers (Hueys) flew in and landed. We could hear them before we were able to see them. The rapid thump-thump-thump bass sound of the turbine-driven rotor blades was distinctive and instantly recognizable. It was a sound that we would become very familiar with for the next year. The Hueys were flying in a long straight line as if they were tied together on a long wire.

Our training had prepared us for the required steps to board quickly and safely. Wait a safe distance back from the landing spot, fasten your helmet with a chin strap, hold your rifle securely with one hand, keep one hand free to grab a bar or seat in the chopper, crouch down slightly to avoid the rotor blades, run forward quickly, jump on, and move to the center. We had all practiced this sequence with stationary helicopters or stripped-down models that had been damaged in combat. This was my first real experience with a helicopter that would be moving fast, pausing briefly to allow me and my buddies to board. I wanted to get it right.

A squadron of Hueys arrive at the water plant for the morning "commute."

A tank from the 11th Armored Cavalry that assisted
in the defense of the water plant.

When they landed on the field, we waited for our helicopter to stop moving then raced forward. The noise was louder than I expected, and the spinning blades stirred up a small tornado of dirt, grass, and dust that forced me to squint as I started moving. I jumped on, sat on the bench and grabbed something to hang onto as the chopper took off again. The entire loading process from the moment the chopper paused on the ground until it started to rise took about six seconds. There were no doors and no seat belts. It was an exciting start to the trip, but there was more to come.

Initially, the chopper rose straight up as it climbed ten or twelve feet off the ground. Then the nose of the craft leaned forward like a charging bull as it accelerated rapidly, gaining both altitude and forward speed. I could feel the vibration increase as the pilot forced the engine to work even harder to get us airborne. The cacophony was overwhelming, with the combination of the turboshaft engine, main rotor, tail rotor, and rushing wind all blending into a massive roar. The only way to communicate was to shout into the ear of the soldier next to you.

There was also a faint smell of kerosene coming from the fuel providing power to the engine. Hueys used JP-4, which was a 50/50 mixture of kerosene and gasoline. After a few minutes we had reached a safer altitude, and the pilot leveled the craft as we continued to climb and move forward over the ground. This was the first helicopter ride of my life, and I have to admit that it was a thrill, a real adrenaline rush.

We were flying along a few thousand feet above the ground looking out over the countryside. Most of the ground below was wet and green and marshy. The rivers looked like travel posters for the Orient, with the twists and curves resembling dragons swaying back and forth looking for victims. We passed over roads and villages that seemed to get smaller and less frequent as we traveled farther inland. Eventually, there were no roads and no villages, just a morass of wet green fields surrounded by palm trees and thick green growth on the edge of each stream and inlet.

Ahead in the distance we saw the faint color of purple smoke in a field. This was our landing zone. A new concern raced through my mind. This would be my first helicopter landing in a combat zone, and I knew that this was one of the most dangerous parts of the mission. Viet Cong soldiers could be waiting in the grass or along the edges of the fields for the choppers to come into range. Hueys are large targets, especially at close range. We and the enemy knew that the choppers would have to slow down to let us out, and for a few agonizingly long seconds, it would be very easy to spray the craft and its occupants with rifles, machine guns, and other weapons. I was frightened but knew that the only path to safety was to move as fast as I could, once we got close to the ground.

The door gunners on both sides of the helicopter checked their M-60 machine guns one more time as we dipped toward the field. They were ready to spray the fields with their guns at the rate of five hundred rounds per minute to discourage the enemy from raising their heads. It turned out that we did not need their help. Another platoon had landed there just before ours and signaled the pilots with smoke grenades on where to land. The area appeared to be secure, so we were able to land in relative safety.

Our ride had lasted only fifteen minutes, although it seemed much longer. We then touched down on the first rice paddy I had ever seen in my life. The landing took place even faster than the boarding procedure. The chopper slowed down as it approached the field and hovered briefly, just barely touching the ground. We quickly jumped off, exiting both sides of the helicopter. Then we raced the thirty yards or so to the outer edges of the field. Once again we bowed our heads to avoid the spinning blades and squinted to try to see through the storm of straw, dirt, and moisture that was being stirred up. By the time we had reached the perimeter, the helicopters had taken off at a steep forward angle and climbed away into the safety of altitude and the sky.

The procedure for starting the ground patrol was always the same. After quickly confirming that everyone was on the ground safely, the platoon proceeded to move out of the field in the direction that we had been assigned to cover for the day. An experienced member of the platoon, who was assigned to be the point man, would start moving forward. We all followed quietly, observing noise discipline and trying to maintain a safe distance so that we did not bunch up and create an inviting target. Conversely, we did not want to lose contact with the lead elements of this patrol, so we were careful not to get too far behind. As one of the new guys, I was assigned a position in the middle of the file where I was less likely to miss something or get lost while I was learning how to function in this new environment.

During the missions we worked in areas consisting of rice paddies lying under six inches of water, as well as tall grass and jungle located along the riverbanks. Moving through a rice paddy was slow, tedious, miserable work. It was bad enough walking through water, but underneath the water there was twelve inches of mud so that every step was like pulling a suction cup off the bottom of your foot. The best analogy was walking with twenty-five-pound weights on each foot. Every time we stopped moving, we had to get down and sit, squat, or kneel in the mud. In order to cross from one paddy to another, we went through a canal roughly six feet across and five feet deep. We held our breath, lifted our weapons up in the air, and waded across.

The extremely flat terrain in this part of Vietnam created a frustrating visibility problem. As we moved through a field, the tall grass, sometimes tall enough to be named elephant grass, made it hard to distinguish fellow soldiers moving through the same field. The fields always seemed to be surrounded by thicker and taller bushes, palm trees, and other vegetation, since they were closer to streams or rivers, making it impossible to see into the next field, where danger might be lurking in front of us or on the left or right of us. Small groups were sent out to move parallel to us on our flanks to warn us of an impending ambush. We proceeded slowly and cautiously.

We crossed four or five rivers that day. In the beginning, I'd sometimes sink into mud up to my chest, and a couple of times it took two men to pull me out. The more experienced troops seemed to move more smoothly and not get stuck as often. I gradually got better at avoiding the straight muddy slopes and searched to the left and right for some stiff bushes or tree roots to provide support through the gray muddy muck. I had thought that I was in good physical shape but found myself exhausted by midmorning.

Half an hour after getting out of a mud hole, I brushed through some bushes and disturbed a nest of red ants that attacked my back, chest, arms, and face. Those damn things bite! I ripped off my gear and my shirt and killed the ants on my chest and face, and a buddy got the ants on my back. Fortunately, there was no permanent damage, no scratches or marks, just a sharp, intense memory of the fact that I had invaded their space.

We took frequent breaks of a few minutes' duration throughout the day. It was an opportunity to swallow another salt tablet or take a couple of sips of water. Our dark-green canteens were made from a stiff plastic, probably cheaper than metal canteens, but more important, they did not make any sound if a rifle butt brushed against them while on patrol.

We moved continuously throughout the day, with a stop around noon for lunch after setting up security facing out in all directions. The C-rations were packaged in small metal cans painted an olive-drab color. Our trusty P-38 can opener, a small (inch and a half) item, did its job effectively. Each C-ration included some type of meat such as ham and eggs, chopped beans and wieners, boned chicken, or ham and lima beans, and a second can with either bread or crackers. The final item on the menu was a fruit-like cocktail, peaches, or pears, or a dessert such as fruit cake, pound cake, or pecan roll. Every C-ration also included an accessory pack with a plastic spoon, salt, pepper, instant coffee, sugar, powdered creamer, gum, cigarettes (four in a pack), matches, and toilet paper. The meals could be eaten cold, but they tasted better if they were heated. If we felt we were in a relatively safe situation, we would use the matches to burn the box the "Cs" came in to heat the meat can.

21

Helicopters ferry troops over the serpentine rivers northeast of Saigon to a drop-off point for a search and destroy mission.

A platoon moves cautiously through a small river inlet while on patrol.

The author struggles through thick mud after an ebb tide drained the water at a crossing point.

Some members of the patrol also carried small white bricks of C-4 explosive, a putty-like material that was safe to carry or drop. It would not explode until a fuse was placed in the brick and detonated. They'd break off a piece and light it to produce a good, clean-burning flame that quickly heated the food in the cans. Cooking fuel was probably an expensive use of explosive material. I estimated that in the course of a year, we probably used only 20 percent of our C-4 requisitions for blowing up tunnels and bunkers. The rest went to heat our meals in the field.

After lunch, we policed the area, buried the used cans in the mud, and picked up all wrappers and any evidence of our presence at this location. We continued the patrol for the rest of the day. We did not find any evidence of VC activity on this mission.

In the late afternoon, the commander received word that the choppers would be half an hour early. Everybody moved over to the pickup zone, but our squad leader forgot to tell three of us, who were still on the outer perimeter of the field. He finally realized that we weren't in the pickup zone, and he yelled across to us to get over there in five minutes, because the choppers were heading in. Well, we ran, plodded, slopped, and crawled across that field and made it just in time. We were pissed at the squad leader, but he just shrugged it off. We boarded quickly, and the choppers took off. It was a quick ride back, and we returned to our hootches at the water plant.

We cleaned up and changed into dry clothes, paying special attention to applying foot powder, and stepped into dry socks. We headed over to the mess area for a hot meal. After the meal, I tried to write a short letter, but I was exhausted and quickly fell asleep.

We continued with the same routine for three more days. The Hueys picked us up every morning, we hiked through the fields, mud, and rivers all day, and they flew us back to our base camp in the late afternoon. We started to feel like commuters. We needed to wake up early and grab breakfast, so we wouldn't miss the 07:00

commuter flight to work. The helicopter rides were the best part of the day, especially the flights back to the water plant.

During this period we did not have any enemy contact or find any rockets. We did have some success on one of the missions. We found a couple of bunkers, fifty pounds of rice, and a couple of AK-47s. We blew up the bunkers and the rice and confiscated the rifles. The area we were patrolling was about six miles north of Saigon. Charlie, a nickname for the Viet Cong, was out there, we just hadn't found him yet.

One afternoon we returned a bit early and had some free time after cleaning up and eating. I was feeling tough and confident and wanted to record this moment in my life, so I passed my camera to a buddy and asked him to take my picture with all my gear on.

He dutifully held the camera, while I overdosed on weapons. I put on two machine gun belts and crisscrossed them Pancho Villa style. I added an M-16 rifle in my right hand and perched an M-60 machine gun on my left shoulder and supported the barrel with my left hand. The coup de grace was a long hunting knife that I clenched between my teeth.

My buddy took the photo. This was intended to be my "badass" photo. I wanted to look tough and mean. Unfortunately, I happened to be smiling when the picture was taken, so I wound up looking like some rookie who had just arrived in-country and didn't really understand what was going on. The picture accurately reflected the fact that I really did have a lot to learn. In the coming weeks, my buddies would teach me.

On Thursday July 18, we stayed in camp and cleaned weapons. In the evening, four of us were sent to a bridge over the Dong Son River up near Long Binh. We were acting as FOs (forward observers), and our job was to call in to HQ and notify them of any flashes that looked like enemy mortars or rockets. We rotated shifts, so that two of us were always awake and alert. The bridge itself was well defended with infantry from the 9th Division; tanks from the 11th Armored Cavalry and a whole compound of ARVNs (Army of the Republic of Vietnam). The VC fired rockets periodically toward Saigon and the surrounding military compounds. We tried to identify the source of the firing, but the enemy kept moving the launch sites. Other units may have been able to identify a location for the launch sites, but on this night, we did not see or hear anything.

We finally got a break on Friday, July 19, when we had a stand-down. This was an opportunity to clean our weapons thoroughly, pick up new gear, and rest. It also provided an opportunity to write letters and keep up with family and my fiancée. Despite its bad reputation, I thought the army food was pretty good. We got a hot breakfast and a hot dinner in the evening as well as sandwiches for lunch when we were in the base camp. As time went on, I started to find time to take some pictures.

The next day we resumed patrols and continued with our search and destroy missions. We were not always in the muddy fields. Some of the patrols were closer to our base camp, so we took trucks to our drop-off point in the morning. We moved through several rubber plantations. They appeared to be safer, because there were fewer places for an enemy to hide. The trees were planted in neat rows extending a great distance. They were neatly trimmed at the bottom, with foliage at the top. You could look directly down a row and see clearly almost to the end of the plantation. If you looked to the left or right at a forty-five-degree angle, you could also see straight through for a great distance. The plantations were established many years ago by the French when they operated as a colonial power. Rubber was an important export from Vietnam and helped to fund the administration of the country.

One warm and quiet evening, I took a few minutes to write a letter. Suddenly the platoon sergeant shouted at a group of us who were nearby. He had a startling announcement. It turned out that Popeye has gotten the hell beaten out of him by a brute named Hunky Dory. The unusual thing about this incident was the fact that, according to the platoon sergeant, this was the first time that Popeye had been beaten in the fourteen years that *Stars and Stripes*, the army newspaper, had carried the strip. The platoon sergeant, Sergeant Moore, was normally a gruff, serious individual not given to small talk, so we were all surprised at his reaction to the cartoon. I made a mental note to avoid making disparaging remarks about any cartoon character.

A note about Sergeant Moore. He was really a remarkable man, tough and very knowledgeable about what was going on in Vietnam. Thirty-eight, a big husky guy with rusty brownish-red hair, he looked like a big Scotsman. This was his second tour in Vietnam. He was supposed to have a desk job, but the army changed priorities, and he landed here with us in a line platoon. Everyone had the utmost confidence in him.

We held a brief memorial service the next day for a soldier from our company who was shot a month ago on the same day that I arrived in Vietnam. I didn't know why they waited so long, but it seemed they usually waited two or three weeks for a service here, so the guys wouldn't be too involved or emotional with the immediacy of the event.

I finished the letter to my fiancée, Christina, that I'd started on the night of Sergeant Moore's outburst. I responded to her question about why we didn't visit Saigon if we were operating very close to the city. The city itself was off-limits to the men of the 1st Infantry Division, because a year or so earlier several men from the Big Red One tore Saigon apart and severely wrecked several bars and hotels and injured several civilians. There were still some men, however, who did venture into the city in spite of this restriction. They took their Big Red One patches off their sleeves and kept their mouths shut.

A few nights later, I found myself sitting on the middle of a bridge at an observation post and facing some strong winds. A storm was coming, and we were sure to be soaked with rain before the night was over. About two thousand meters downstream, there were two helicopter gunships firing at some enemy or suspected enemy position. It was a long distance away, so we didn't hear the sound. It was dark, so all we could see were the red tracers as they raced to the ground. The scene could almost be viewed as artistic, with the red tracers silhouetted against the black night sky, if it weren't for the fact that someone might be killed in the encounter.

Shortly after, a truck drove by and fired a couple of rounds in the air (not at us). The company in charge of safeguarding the bridge pulled them over at the end of the bridge and searched them. They turned out to be a couple of drunken ARVNs, who often fired their weapons randomly without any specific target.

Our job was to report to our headquarters VC mortar or rocket flashes along with the compass direction and estimated distance. Other observation posts in other areas were doing the same thing. If HQ got two or more reports at the same time, they were able to draw lines on a map and look at the point of intersection, which was the most likely position of the VC rockets. Then the position was targeted for search and destroy missions.

The next day we went through and checked out two small villages. It wasn't a thorough search, we were just sort of keeping tabs on the situation. Before we were picked up in the afternoon, I saw an unusual plant in a spot where we had halted temporarily. It looked like a small fern. When I touched its leaves, they folded up instantly. When I tapped the stem, all of the leaves folded up, and the entire plant drooped over as if dead. If left alone, it raised itself and opened up again in three to five minutes. Perhaps it was related to the Venus flytrap. This was one of the advantages of being in an infantry unit. We spent a lot of time on the ground and had the opportunity to get up close and personal with nature.

We returned to the water plant just as the rains started. I spent an hour drying out my hootch. We were now in the monsoon season, although the rain hadn't been too bad so far. That night was an exception, because it poured in solid walls of water for two hours. There was a six-inch layer of water on the ground surrounding the water plant before it finally started to drain off. There were two of us living in my hootch, but my hootchmate, Cid, had just left on a seven-day leave to Hawaii to get married (I'm not sure how he managed that feat), so I did the cleanup.

The next day we headed out on another patrol. We'd normally fly either north or south of Saigon, but that day we flew right over it. It was a sprawling city with many large and small rivers, numerous ships, and dozens of bridges. It reminded me of New York City, only without the skyscrapers. It was an impressive sight!

After getting dropped off in our landing zone, we spent the day patrolling along a river. We had no enemy contact and found no evidence of rockets. It rained all afternoon, and we grew more miserable. We were soaking wet, sitting in rice paddies filled with a sea of mud. Every step that day saw us moving through mud and water.

Later that day one of the men in the left file stepped into a punji pit. This was a low-cost booby trap that the Viet Cong constructed to injure and slow down American soldiers. It consisted of sticks that were one or two feet long sharpened to a point at the end. The pointed sticks were jammed, at an angle, into the dirt in the sides of a hole that was perhaps two feet deep. The pit was then covered with leaves and other vegetation to conceal the location. When a soldier stepped into the pit, the stakes would penetrate the leg, especially if he tried to move or pull his leg out.

Our point man had missed it, but this guy didn't. One of the stakes went through the side of his boot about an inch into his leg. He pulled the stake out then removed his leg from the pit without further injury. He put some antiseptic on it and continued with us for the rest of the afternoon. He could have been taken out by a medevac helicopter, but he said that it didn't hurt. The medics checked it thoroughly when we got back and confirmed he was OK.

Late in the afternoon we found a VC grenade tied to a stake with a piece of string that stretched over to a nearby bush. One of our men tied a line around the string and handed it to me as everyone stood back and got down. I pulled the line, but the grenade failed to go off. We then attached a small amount of C-4 explosive and blew it in place.

We returned to the water plant, had some food, and cleaned up. The chaplain stopped by in the evening to say mass, and several of us attended the service. I had not experienced any really close calls in the field so far, but I knew that we were in a dangerous line of work. I didn't believe that God was on our side. God didn't really choose sides in wars. In my theology classes, I had studied the concept of the "just war" that allowed Catholics to fight in a war that would prevent or stop an injustice. This conflict was confusing. The Church had not declared that this war was unjust, although a significant number of theologians and religious leaders publicly held the opposite belief. I also struggled with the legitimacy of killing. The fifth commandment seemed pretty clear. It did not include a list of exceptions. I had, however, studied a broader interpretation in religion classes. I hoped these interpretations were correct. In the circumstances I found myself in, I felt a need to reinforce my faith as well as my belief that I was doing the right thing. The priest tried to make it to the water plant every Tuesday night. I tried to attend the service when I could.

The next morning I was introduced to another one of the delights of Vietnam. This one was called bamboo poisoning. My left forearm was very itchy the night before, and when I awoke in the morning, I had five blisters on my arm, each about half an inch long. The medic put some ointment on and said to be careful not to break them, because they would leave scars. He said the stuff is similar to poison ivy, because it comes from contact with some plant. They weren't certain that it was caused by bamboo, but they called it that for want of a better name.

We headed out on a mission the next day and were told that there was a possibility that we might make contact. We were revisiting a VC base camp that had been discovered the previous month, and at that time more than a hundred rockets were found. We went through the camp carefully and found no new signs of occupancy or activity. We blew up six bunkers that were still intact after the last visit. In the afternoon it rained again, but it wasn't too bad because we didn't have too far to go, and the ground was relatively solid with only four to six inches of mud.

I received another new assignment which was a four-hour night shift on guard duty at the top of the water tower. The top of the tower was about 140 feet high and accessed by a long climb up a metal ladder attached to the inside wall of the tower. On reaching the top, I relieved the other guard, who headed down. I could hear the eerie sound of rushing water through large pipes that were contained inside the tower. They were designed to maintain powerful pressure to meet the water needs of the citizens of Saigon.

I was equipped with a compass, binoculars, and a landline phone. My mission was to scan the horizon and call in flashes from rockets or mortars. The terrain around the water plant was very flat and only a few feet above sea level, so I was able to see a great distance and respond to the calls for a "sit-rep," a situation report, every half hour. It was a quiet night, and there were no rocket flashes to be seen. At the end of my shift, I climbed down the ladder and headed to my hootch to get some sleep before our new patrol the next morning.

A few days later I was assigned to the trash detail—a quick, easy job. We loaded the trash from our camp into a trailer and then rode in the jeep, hauling the trailer a short distance to a nearby dump site located outside the camp. We would bring our weapons but didn't expect to need them to protect the trash. As we began unloading the trailer, at least a dozen children showed up from a nearby village and start going through the items as we dropped them off. They ranged in age from five to ten and were evenly divided between boys and girls. They were accompanied by a small brown-and-white dog that was also searching for food scraps. The first time I saw the children, I was struck by their presence there.

Vietnamese children dig through fresh trash from our base, looking for C-rations, empty sandbags, and anything else that was salvageable.

One of the 105 mm howitzers that assisted in the defense of the water plant.

I had seen pictures of children searching through trash in newspaper stories about refugee camps in different parts of the world, but this was the first time that I had seen them with my own eyes.

The trash was the assorted detritus of an army camp: cardboard boxes, empty cardboard tubes that had held mortar shells, empty wooden ammo boxes, Coke cans, and milk cartons. The children, though poor by our standards, were neat and clean and reasonably well dressed. The boys wore shorts and plain short-sleeved shirts. The girls wore white blouses and black pants. Some of the boys wore the soft caps with a brim that our soldiers wore for light-duty tasks. The girls all had a plastic headband or barrette in their hair. The men in our detail were wearing jungle boots with thick soles to protect their feet. The children wore a simple pair of sandals as they stepped through the piles of boxes and rubbish.

They picked through each item and examined it carefully to determine its value and use. One girl found an unopened can from a C-ration box. A boy found a piece of clear plastic sheeting. Another girl picked up a can of peanuts that still had some nuts in the bottom, the remnants of a soldier's gift box sent from his family. A tall girl about nine years old recovered a sleeve of crackers in a plastic wrapper that was still half-full.

The boys lifted the heavier items and searched for items of interest underneath the debris. The girls moved more cautiously but deliberately as they methodically checked each item. There was a quiet dignity in their movements. We finished unloading the trailer and drove back to the water plant.

# CHAPTER 3

# FELLOW SOLDIERS—CAMARADERIE AND DIVERSITY

Our daily patrols continued through wet fields. On Friday, July 26, we moved through a VC base camp that another company had destroyed a month earlier. The VC had not returned, but I picked up a souvenir, a long banner on which was handwritten a Vietnamese slogan, "Toàn dãn hãy đừng lên vợ trận khối nhà cũng với quận Đối cách-manc tiêu diệt ciac mỹ và bọn việt cian bạn nước. Thiếu-Kỹ-Loạn." Years later a Vietnamese friend provided me with the translation: "Fellow citizens, we are the people who will be standing up, in spirit, in arms with the People's Revolutionary Army, we will defeat, we will wipe them out, the bullies American, and their puppets, the traitors, Thieu, Ky, Loan."

Thieu was president of South Vietnam. Ky was vice president. Loan was the police chief who shot a Viet Cong suspect in the head with a revolver while a press photographer took the photo that shocked the world.

Sometimes even a grunt gets lucky. My lucky day was Saturday, July 27. I spent the whole day swimming. When we searched a river, we had four men in the water, and a file of troops on each side of the river. On that day, I was one of the guys in the river. I was a reasonably good swimmer, having learned to swim as a kid in a public pool in New York City. As a teenager, I spent eight summers working on Brighton Beach in Brooklyn selling Good Humor ice cream and had plenty of opportunities to swim in the ocean in my free time.

Teams of two swimmers covered each side of the river. My partner and I had the right side. We wore our pants rolled up and a T-shirt to prevent sunburn. We rigged two air mattresses connected with a short rope. Our weapons, helmets, boots, and all the rest of our gear were placed on the rear air mattress. One of us lay on the other air mattress and floated along the river's edge. The other man swam close to the riverbank and checked for caves, rockets, sampans, and other items of interest. We switched every half hour—one man on the raft and the other moving along the riverbank. Every time a river branched or split, we helped the company get across by setting up a rope between each bank and ferrying the machine guns and radios across on the air mattresses.

On this day, the only thing we found was a fifteen-foot wooden boat. The VC had hidden it on the bottom of the river about fifteen feet from the riverbank and chained it down in about seven feet of water. We raised the boat, pushed it into the middle of the river, and blew it up with a grenade. We then continued searching the riverbanks until the end of the day.

We returned to the water plant, changed our clothes, and headed for the mess area. After eating I wrote a letter to my younger brother, Gary, and enclosed some Vietnamese currency, a twenty-piaster bill, equal to about seventeen cents in American money. The exchange rate was 118 piasters for a dollar. Most of the Vietnamese money was paper currency worth so many Ps, or piasters. They had three coins called dongs; the one dong, five dong, and ten dong. A dong is equal to a piaster, so a five-dong coin was equal to five piasters. They called them dongs and piasters to differentiate between coins and paper. I had asked my family to send me some snack items and a couple dozen long candles. We used these twelve-inch candles to light up the inside of our hootches at night, so we could read or write letters. The Viet Cong knew we were there at the water plant, and it was a pretty big target, so the candlelight from our hootches was not giving our position away.

That day was also a lucky day for another reason. Every three days we received an SP box. The SP stands for sundries pack. We got the box and divided it up among the twenty-five men in our platoon. The box contained twenty rolls of Lifesavers; twenty-four packs of Chuckles; seventy-two Hershey bars; seventy-two packs of M&M's; seventy-two assorted (Tootsie Rolls; caramels, etc); a hundred packets of chewing gum; two pens; three packs of envelopes; three packs of writing paper; ten cartons of cigarettes; three boxes of pipe tobacco; one packet of chewing tobacco; a hundred packs of matches; one razor; two cans of shaving cream; three toothbrushes; eight tubes of toothpaste; twelve packs of razor blades (Gillette); a box of pipe cleaners; two packs of cigars; twelve bars of soap, and twenty rolls of Charms. Since all of these items were free, there was never a shortage of candy, cigarettes, or soap.

The routine of patrols while searching for VC and rockets continued. On Sunday, July 28, I realized that I had been in Vietnam for a month. We'd go out for three days and generally have a stand-down on the fourth day to clean weapons and ammunition, read, rest, and relax. We were always busy, but it helped the time go by. I was now getting enough sleep, and I was lucky to have a great bunch of guys in my unit. I had thought the first month whizzed by; if every month went by this fast, I'd be home in no time.

We were a pretty close-knit group, and I felt accepted for who I was with no pretensions. The way to be accepted was to simply do your job and pull your share of the load. If you did that, everyone was happy because every extra man meant another rifle that might save your life and another person to share the daily burden. It may sound a little callous, but that was basically what it boiled down to. Everybody wanted to keep every other member of the group motivated and engaged, so there was a lot of joking around and a lot of horseplay.

We would have discussions about a variety of topics, especially in the early evening when everyone was still awake. Usually the conversation focused on familiar themes such as families back home, girls, cars, sports teams, food, etc. There was not a lot of talk about politicians or government policies. Most of us would have preferred a quick end to the war but didn't view that as likely to happen soon. Everyone understood that there was a personal contract with the army and the government. Once we were in Vietnam, we knew we had a 365-day contract to stay there. At the end of that time, we would be free to return to the United States either for discharge or a stateside assignment. As a result, everyone had a short-term focus. Get through this day, then the next day. When we reached a monthly anniversary, we'd tear another month off the calendar and recalculate the number of days left.

As civilians, many of us had participated in lengthy discussions about the reasons for the war. There were many aspects of the war and various leaders we might have criticized. It was one thing to discuss war policy in the abstract. It was something very different to be an active participant. Now that we were living with the day-to-day reality, our focus changed to survival. We wanted to get through this experience without being wounded or killed.

There was generally a strong level of camaraderie in spite of significant differences in age, background, and education. Some were in their late teens and some of us were "old" guys at twenty-three. Some were fresh out of high school, and some of us had been to college. We were from five general geographic regions: the Northeast, the Deep South, the Midwest, Texas, and California. I tried not to judge people based on stereotypes, but in many cases, some strong images did come through. The guys from the South and Texas were generally the most gung ho, and many were eager to make contact with the enemy and do their duty. The men from the Midwest were the most even tempered and wanted to get through each day, so they could return to their homes and families. The Northeast segment tended to be the most liberal, harboring more negative views of the war and questioning our reasons for being there. Many of the Californians really did seem to have come from another planet. They were laid-back and mellow and didn't seem to care about anything that was going on. Many were also eager to try some of the milder drugs available in the larger villages. At this stage of the war (1968–69) few of us wanted to take a chance of being less than 100 percent alert when we went on patrol, although this outlook changed in the years that followed.

The stereotypes I've just mentioned were generalizations and my personal perceptions. As with all generalizations, there were exceptions. There were serious, thoughtful Southerners, gung ho Northeast natives, and bright, intelligent Californians who were members of our company.

The fact was that this group of young men with such diverse backgrounds did want to work together with a common goal: getting back in one piece. As long as each of us did his job responsibly, we earned the respect of every other man. The irony of the situation was that the US Army, probably one of the most rigid and hierarchical organizations on earth, was a great teacher of democracy and teamwork. Each man was judged on the basis of his skill and his willingness to help the others when the situation required it.

It had been a long, tiring day tramping through elephant grass, as tall as a man, along a shallow muddy river. That night I was an acting FO on the bridge with three other men. I wrote a letter to Christina by flashlight while it was my turn to monitor the radio and talked about the experiences of the day. She replied some time later that the letters, combined with the pictures I was sending, helped her to understand what I was going through.

Later that week, I had my first experience with leeches. We had stopped midmorning to set up a secure perimeter after going through some wet ditches. I felt something on my chest and opened my shirt. Three leeches were attached to my skin. My first inclination was to pull them off, but we had been warned not to do this. I noticed that several other guys were also removing leeches. Some used a lit cigarette to make the leeches drop off. I used my insect repellent. I squirted a small amount on the first leech, and it dropped off. I repeated the process for the second and third. They left small marks where they broke the skin, but there were no long-term ill effects.

Leeches and red ants would be our frequent companions during our tour. They were fairly minor annoyances that were inconsequential by themselves, but combined with heat, humidity, exhaustion, and fear of enemy phantoms that fired at us and disappeared, they became major annoyances. The worst experience with red ants actually occurred in February when we set up for an ambush along a berm just after sunset. We were only there for a few minutes when we realized that the entire length of the berm was one giant red-ant colony. We couldn't see the ants, but we felt them nipping at us. The entire platoon moved to a new location, got into position, and spent the next hour trying to remove the ants, manually crushing each section of our bodies until most of them were gone. Several guys shared the view that we should have joined the navy.

On a happier note, I completed my application for R&R (rest and recuperation) in Australia, Tokyo, or Hong Kong—in that order. We were advised not to apply for Hawaii unless we were meeting our wives there. There was such a long waiting list for Hawaii that many married men, who were given priority, could not get over there. R&R worked on a quota system, with so many slots going to each unit. I applied for the month of January because I'd have more seniority then. The air transportation was free both ways, so I wanted to take advantage of this opportunity. If I didn't get Australia, I'd still be happy with one of the alternates.

We spent another day on a search and destroy mission, but the only thing we destroyed was grass, which we burned anytime we found it growing tall on rice paddy dikes. This prevented VC from using the dikes as firing positions.

Every day, the company left one man behind to guard the hootches and mortars and to clean up the place. It was my turn. It was a good deal, because you didn't go into the field, and you only had to work for about three hours. Then you could sleep or read for the rest of the day. I slept for a few hours and then started reading a new book.

It was cool and breezy in the evening, and it looked like it was going to rain. In spite of all the rain and mud we dealt with, we did not have to live in wet fatigues. We got a dry pair every night right after chow.

They called my hootchmate Cid, because when he first joined the unit, everyone suspected him of being a detective. Military detectives were called CID (an abbreviation of the formal US Army

Criminal Investigation Command). Even though he wasn't in the military police, the name stuck. When I first arrived, I thought his name was a reference to the Spanish military character and literary figure, El Cid.

Cid returned from Hawaii. We found out the trip was charged as a seven-day emergency leave, but he managed to stay out of the field a few more days by killing time in airports and division headquarters and various transfer points. While he was gone, I improved our hootch by putting a plastic door on his side which had been leaking. The plastic kept our space nice and dry.

Someone ordered too much ice cream in the artillery unit attached to our company, so that evening they went around the camp passing out half gallons of vanilla, chocolate, and strawberry. There was more than enough, which was a surprising treat. In the evening I gathered my gear and got ready to spend the night on the bridge as an observer watching for rockets.

It was always great to receive packages in the field. Since the army post office now had my permanent address, my family and fiancée were able to send packages on a regular basis. One of the first was from my father, containing cookies, brownies, a field knife, and a compass. I appreciated everything.

The following day, we had our second medevac chopper in as many days. Medevac was military shorthand for medical evacuation, which was usually done by helicopters painted with a red cross. A guy in my platoon had been stung in the face several times by bumblebees. He was feeling sick and dizzy after that, so they took him out. That may seem like a strange reason to use an expensive helicopter for one man, but the bumblebees were the size of golf balls, so it was like getting bitten by a small bird or rodent. Fortunately, he was OK the next day.

The next day a man in my platoon hurt his back while trying to cross a river with a rope. We suspected he slipped a disc; he was in great pain. We made a litter for him with a poncho and some bamboo poles and carried him to a nearby field, where a medevac helicopter took him out. I had my camera with me and used the last three shots on my roll of black-and-white film to record the incident.

A few days later we had a stand-down, and I spent most of the day cleaning my weapon and my magazines. Around noon, the first sergeant came up to our platoon for a short detail that required three men. I was one of the men chosen for this mission.

We grabbed our rifles and ammo and ran out to the chopper pad, where a Huey was waiting to take off. We jumped on and started flying. There were already three demolition experts from another unit on the chopper. The mission was to locate and destroy three bomb cluster containers. Each container was about ten feet long and looked like a big bomb. They were carried by jets and held a large number of small bombs, each about the size of a pint beer bottle. Somehow the containers fell from the planes and failed to detonate. We had to find them.

We flew around for an hour in an area of about eight square miles. We finally located all three containers. We landed at each bomb site, and three of us infantry types deployed to the rear and two sides of the landing zone to provide security. The three demolition men went to the front, set a time charge, and returned to the chopper. We all got back on the chopper, took off, and circled the field until the bomb blew up. We did this three times until each bomb was neutralized. The entire mission took two hours. We flew back to our camp when it was over. One thing about the army, it was not a typical nine-to-five job.

Another morning when we had a stand-down, I was assigned to help provide an escort for the supply truck that was heading to Thu Duc, the largest city in our area and the provincial capital. This was actually a pretty good duty assignment, since it meant that another

A wounded soldier is placed on a stretcher and carried to a Medevac chopper that will quickly fly him to a hospital for treatment.

soldier and I would be stationed on the bed of the open-top two-and-a-half-ton truck also known as a "deuce and a half."

Our job was to defend the driver, the truck, and the load, in the event that the Viet Cong tried to attack us while driving on the open highway. Trucks and convoys had been attacked numerous times over the past few years, but not in the last few months. Our load that day was a truck full of dirty fatigues. We were prepared to defend this load of laundry with our lives. It was an uneventful run, and we made it to the laundry without incident. The Viet Cong were not able to cripple the American war effort by capturing our dirty laundry that day.

The laundry facility itself was impressive. It was a steel-frame building, nearly three stories high, that took up almost a full city block. We helped the driver unload the truck and took the contents to a long wooden counter at the entrance, where three young, smiling Vietnamese women filled out the brief paperwork and handed the driver a receipt. Then they brought several stacks of clean, folded fatigues, which we loaded in the truck.

The activity in the building behind the counter was energetic. Long rows of commercial washers, dryers, and pressing units were being used by a small army of Vietnamese women and a few older men. Some Vietnamese entrepreneur had won a contract from Uncle Sam to clean our laundry. He would probably continue to make a lot of money as long as the war continued.

After loading the clean laundry, we boarded the truck, drove a short distance to a small shop, and bought a couple of bottles of Coke. The driver chose this vendor because his Cokes were packed in ice. We drove back to the base and spent some time cleaning our weapons.

On Tuesday, August 6, I lucked out again with an assignment to go swimming while checking riverbanks. The river was deeper and wider and cleaner than usual and was moving rapidly. The fast-moving water also meant fewer mosquito bites, which was fine with me. We managed to get through the day without any enemy contact. To be precise, we had no active enemy contact. We did discover an enemy grave that we dug up. We found the decomposed remains of a Viet Cong. We dug up graves out in the boonies, because the VC would often bury weapons, mortars, or ammunition in the ground and make it look like a grave.

The weather was still warm, although it rained every afternoon. I was told that it was a relatively dry monsoon season, with not nearly as much rain as they usually had at that time of year.

On Wednesday, August 7, we set up for a night ambush along the side of a highway near the water plant. In addition to our normal weapons and gear, one of the soldiers in our platoon was assigned to bring a starlight scope. This was a special night scope that weighed about six pounds and could be handheld or mounted on top of an M-16 rifle. It amplified existing light from the moon, stars, or ambient light in the sky. You peered through the scope and saw a green image with dark outlines. Flat terrain or sky showed up as bright green, while trees, animals, and people appeared as black objects. It did not work on nights with total darkness, because it needed some light source to operate. The scope was also used on guard towers in base camps because of its ability to see people not visible to the naked eye.

During the course of the night, everyone on watch would look for movement and listen for the sounds of movement. We hoped that the person with the starlight scope would provide us with an earlier warning. We settled in for a long night. Everyone in the country knew there was a curfew from 21:00 until dawn. Orders were to shoot anything that moved near the highway after 22:00, but tonight nothing moved. I had been there over a month, and we had yet to make enemy contact. That was fine with me.

The next day we went out on another routine patrol, checking out another VC base camp that had been destroyed some time ago. There were no signs of recent habitation, so we left and continued on.

Just before we broke for chow at noon, one of my buddies found a coconut that was in beautiful shape. We drank the milk and then cracked open the coconut. It was delicious. We had C-rations for lunch, and then we finished up the coconut. It really made the day. The guy who found the coconut was Bob Morrison, a twenty-three-old with two years of college at the University of New Mexico. He was an interesting guy and very sharp. He had a fifteen-year-old brother who was spending the summer in Israel picking peaches on a kibbutz.

My hootchmate, Cid, and Bob were impressed with the packages that I had been receiving from my fiancée. They put a shopping list together and asked if I would include it in one of my letters. I agreed, and this was their request.

"Dear Christina,

We have been completely abandoned by America. We haven't received anything in months. Would you please send us the following items:
Pepperoni (Italian hard sausage), (skinny hard salami)
Salami (hard) will not spoil in mail
Olives (with red centers and green skin)
Send the bill to Steve.

—Bob (with the brother in Israel)
—Cid (Steve's hootchmate)

The items won't spoil in the mail.
PS—Don't worry, we'll take care of naïve boyfriend.
Thank you much."

We had an intensive weapons check one evening. All weapons were thoroughly cleaned and then inspected by the sergeants and officers. Most of the weapons (including mine) passed on the first inspection. After the inspection, mail was passed out. I received another letter from Christina, and she asked if I could read her handwriting. I didn't have any problem reading her letters, except when she sometimes used red ink. All of our flashlights had a red lens to cut down on the emitted light, especially at night in the field. The red light canceled out her red ink, and all I saw was a blank page. I told her that I used candles to read her letters at the camp, so she didn't have to change her ink.

# CHAPTER 4

# SWIMMING FOR RIFLES AND SAMPANS

We set out on a river sweep on Sunday, August 11, and I spent the day swimming in the water. It started out as an exceptional day. I had the opportunity to bring my camera and got some outstanding shots of the river, of the other soldiers and me on the raft, and a couple of bridges that the VC had blown up.

In the late afternoon while checking the bank of a wide river, Bob Morrison and I came to a tributary that flowed into the main river. This main river was two hundred feet across and the tributary was about twenty-five feet across. The file on the left bank had to cross the tributary. I was on the lead air mattress towing a second air mattress with a short length of cord connecting both. The second air mattress carried all of our gear. Bob was near me in the water checking the mud along the bank. I noticed the point man starting to cross the tributary, and I shouted to him to wait until I checked the depth. He said not to worry and started across. The water was up to his shoulders which was not unusual, but I continued swimming while towing the air mattresses toward him in case he needed help. He was almost halfway across when the water rose to the level of his chin, and he kept going. He took another step and disappeared. I was about twenty-five feet away and tore after him, grabbed his shoulder, and pulled him up so that he could hang on to the air mattress. I towed the point man and the two air mattresses to the opposite bank, where he was headed. He was OK.

I looked back in the water and saw Bob diving down in the water. He came up with my camera and my helmet. It seems that when I took off, a lot of gear fell off the air mattress. My camera, helmet, rifle, ammo, boots, and the demolition bag fell off. He recovered my camera, rifle, helmet, ammo, and the demolition bag, but he couldn't find my boots, which were swept away by the current. The film was ruined, but that was the least of my problems. We helped the rest of the platoon finish crossing with the air mattresses and then headed to our pickup zone. Since I had no boots, I wound up walking about a thousand meters in my stocking feet. It had turned out to be an interesting day. I lost a good camera, but nobody was shooting at us. I chalked it up to experience.

The company followed up on the weapons check from the previous night by conducting a live fire check into a dirt bank to confirm that they were all in good mechanical condition. I fired two magazines, about thirty-six rounds. My rifle was in excellent shape, and there was no problem with jamming or anything else.

The following day we went out as a single platoon, while the other three platoons in the company stayed back. It wasn't too bad, because we were on solid ground all day. We went five times farther than we usually did when we traveled in the mud. We went through several small villages and kept checking ID cards and hootches for weapons, etc. Everyone over the age of eighteen, male and female, had to carry an ID card.

A serious incident occurred in the middle of the morning. We had set up a checkpoint along a stretch of road leading into a village. It was my job to check the ID of everyone going into the village, while someone at the other end was checking everyone leaving. There were eight children sitting on the side of the road watching me stop people. They appeared indifferent, but a bit curious. I stopped several people, and the kids remained stone-faced. Many of the Vietnamese rode bicycles and motorbikes like Yamaha, Suzuki, etc. all over the countryside. Many others simply walked from village to village.

Suddenly a motorbike came tearing down the road toward me at full speed. I raised my rifle and stepped into the middle of the road to show him that he needed to stop. I was certain that he saw me, but he didn't slow down. I put my finger on the trigger ready to fire a warning shot, followed by a direct shot if he didn't slow down. I looked carefully to see if he had a weapon or a grenade. I didn't see any, but I was still ready for any sudden move. My adrenaline was racing. He abruptly slowed down and approached slowly on his bike. My rifle was pointed directly at him as he got closer. When he got within fifteen feet I realized that he was only about ten years old. He was not required to carry an ID card, so I had no justification to stop him. I stepped aside and let him pass through. As I started back to the other side of the road, I noticed that all of the kids were laughing and pointing at me. They realized what had happened and were amused at my frustration and confusion. I calmed down and was suddenly thankful that the boy on the bike finally slowed down. If he hadn't, this incident could have had a tragic ending. I understood that I might have to fire at enemy soldiers in the context of a firefight or an ambush. Shooting a ten-year-old boy was not something that I would ever be able to rationalize.

We finished our mission for the day and returned to camp. When we got back we found out that another company in our battalion had contact that day; two of our men were killed, and several were wounded. They made contact in the same location that we had gone through five days earlier. There was also increased nighttime activity, because we could see more flares being fired and more gunships (armed helicopters) firing every night. It looked like the calm period was coming to an end.

The following day helicopters flew us to a field next to a wide river. One disconcerting aspect of our patrols was that most of us had no idea where we were after we landed. The platoon leader and the sergeants had marked the grid coordinates on their maps for our starting and ending locations for the day. Most days, the terrain looked exactly like the terrain from the previous days: wet fields and small rivers bordered by palm trees and bushes. Our area of operation was in a very flat part of the country with no hills or mountains that could be used as landmarks. Unless we were patrolling near a village, we didn't even have a road to follow or use as a reference point. The monotony and anonymity of our surroundings left us eager for something that would change the routine.

We were about to experience just such a change. Our mission was to board several engineer boats (twenty-foot metal boats with outboard motors) and check out the area along the riverbanks. Our platoon was to spend the day in the boats providing fire support if we made contact, but there was a last minute change of plans. As we boarded the boats, the captain decided that he needed two swimmers in the water, and two of us were picked for the job.

Now, I normally liked the swimming job, but I was looking forward to a quiet day sitting in the boat. As it turned out, it was the roughest day of swimming I'd ever had. The water was deep, and the banks were steep, so instead of walking along the riverbank half-submerged, we had to keep swimming. In the afternoon as the tide went out, the river current started to move rapidly in the opposite direction, and I was almost swept downstream a couple of times. There were some bends in the river that were so swift that I was swimming as hard as I could and was still moving backward. At these times the only way I could move forward was to have the motorboat tow me.

We did, however, find twelve sampans buried near the shore. We checked them for weapons, then we set charges and blew them up. It had been a tiring day, but still better than average. In the mid-afternoon we got out of the river and proceeded on foot to finish the patrol and head to our pickup point. While moving we had another medevac case. One of our soldiers was bitten by a snake and was airlifted out. We never heard how he fared, but snakebites were not normally fatal.

We heard and read government reports about "occasional" cases of drug addiction; however, it was more prevalent than we thought. We had a special orientation by the chaplain and a doctor. They emphasized that the stuff over here was stronger than what was sold in the States. They "cut" the stuff in the States, but in Vietnam they sold a pure version. Shortly after the orientation, the company commander caught one of the cooks taking drugs. The cook was a kid about twenty years old who often walked around with a glassy look in his eyes. They took him up to Camp LBJ (It was not named for President Johnson; LBJ was Long Binh Jail).

My fiancée asked me to describe the countryside and the people. The countryside in the immediate area consisted of wet, muddy rice paddies. There were hundreds of rivers and canals of all sizes intertwining and connecting all around the area. The riverbanks were covered with palms, vines, elephant grasses, and other thick vegetation. These jungle-like banks extended for ten meters on either side of the river. There were some dry fields in this area, but they were usually covered with elephant grass five to six feet tall. You couldn't see a man five feet in front of you.

Most individuals we met were young children, older adults (forty-five and up) and women, especially younger women. Most of the kids around the base camps would beg for candy or cigarettes and root through the garbage. They didn't smoke the cigarettes; they sold them, since American cigarettes brought a high price on the black market.

There always seemed to be plenty of young women around in or near our base camps, in villages, or near outposts such as bridges, etc. They were between the ages of fifteen and twenty-five, and many were prostitutes. Some of the guys claimed that every young girl there was a prostitute. I found that hard to believe, although it appeared that a large number of them were. It was a quick and easy way to make money in a nation of uncertainty and turmoil. They called the girls "short-timers" because they slept with men for a short-time. The going rate started at three hundred piasters which was about $2.60 in American money. The girls would approach with a smile and say, "GI, want short-time?" Just outside the wire, about six hundred feet from my hootch, there was a snack cart selling bread and soft drinks. Frequently, the girls would hang out there. At any given time there were two or three guys in the platoon on penicillin.

Life in a combat infantry unit made it hard to keep track of time. There were no weekends; one day passed into the next. We took our malaria pills every Monday, and that was the only way we could tell the day of the week.

I received a package from home, including a box of candles. Since I didn't really stay up very late at night, I only used them for about an hour or two when I didn't have guard duty, so they lasted quite a while.

The temperature was generally pretty warm, but it cooled off at night, so sleeping wasn't too bad. The thing that made it warm during the day was the fact that we were carrying all our gear. While it was summer back in the States, it was winter in Vietnam.

The monsoon rains, which lasted until December, kept things cool. During January and February the rains stopped, and it felt like summer and got very hot.

We went out on a patrol with tracks. Tracks was a nickname for APCs (armored personnel carriers), built like small tanks designed to carry soldiers into combat. Instead of tires, the vehicles moved on tank-like treads called tracks. The tracks stopped every three or four miles when we got off to check out a village. I always brought some candy from our SP packs for the kids in the villages. One benefit was that it kept them happy. Also, you could expect VC to be in the area when the kids didn't ask for candy.

The next night, while our platoon stayed back at the water plant and manned the bunkers and towers, most of the company went out on a village seal. They blew an ambush and killed several VC. The ambush was along a river where several VC were caught as they were going by in a sampan. The village that had been sealed off was checked out the next day and revealed no enemy presence.

The next day we went out on patrol again. One of our guys was carrying a little tin of Excedrin in the band that fastens the camouflage cover to the helmet. At the time there was a series of TV commercials that referenced different types of situations that resulted in headaches, such as Excedrin Headache #742, "The Commuter Train is Late" or Excedrin Headache #253, "Teacher with a Rowdy Class." We should have filmed a new one called Excedrin Headache #476, "The Firefight," army jargon for a mutual exchange of bullets.

We were riding in trucks along the highway when we turned at an intersection and saw a line of five or six Lambrettas parked on the side of the road. They were waiting for more people to meet them.

Lambrettas were three-wheeled vehicles, very popular in Vietnam because they were economical to purchase and operate. There was a single wheel in the front under the driver's seat and two wheels farther back. The design included a small cabin that sat over the rear wheels, with a bench on each side, and a simple frame supporting the roof of the vehicle. They could transport four passengers plus the driver. Occasionally, we saw as many as six passengers. The engine was small, with about the same horsepower as a small motorcycle. This part of Vietnam was very flat, so the low horsepower was well suited to meet the needs of the local population.

We left the trucks when we reached our drop-off point and started walking along a small road near a village. We passed a few civilians going about their daily chores. We met a young girl, perhaps twelve or thirteen years old. She was carrying four large ceramic jugs on a long wooden pole. The pole rested on her right shoulder with ropes attached at both ends. The ropes formed a basket shape that held two of the jugs on each end. The jugs were thick ceramic, weighing at least fifteen pounds. The total load was probably at least sixty pounds.

She seemed to be struggling under the weight, stopping every twenty or thirty feet and shifting the weight to her other shoulder. Her struggle reminded us that many of the people in this area of Vietnam were poor farmers trying to make a living from their small plots of land and making the best of each day in spite of their difficult lives. We seldom heard anyone complain, but we were probably not the best reporters of their feelings and emotions. We were part of a large military intrusion moving through their village or farmland. They simply wanted us to move through quickly and did not want to attract our attention in any way.

We continued past the village for another half hour and came upon a long row of concrete pipe sections along the edge of an open field. Each section of pipe was five feet in diameter and five or six feet long. They were lined up and waiting for a work crew. We believed that they were to be used for a water or sewage pipeline. We checked each section of pipe and found nothing unusual, so we continued on our way.

It was now early in the afternoon, and we were moving through a thick growth of palm trees, bushes, and tall grass in an area so remote and inhospitable that the farmers did not venture out there. The point man spotted an opening in the dirt behind some bushes, so we stopped and surrounded the area. One of the shorter soldiers was assigned the job of "tunnel rat" and crawled into the tunnel to check it out. It was very short, less than ten feet in length, and there were no signs that anyone had ever occupied this tunnel. He crawled back out, and another soldier placed a small amount of C-4 explosive in the entrance and called out as he detonated the charge. The entrance collapsed on itself, and we moved out. The tunnel was the biggest excitement of the day. We did not see any other evidence of Viet Cong activity, so we finished the patrol and advanced to our pickup point before returning to camp.

I sent some more money to my brother, a fifty-piaster bill worth about forty-four US cents and a hundred-piaster bill worth about eighty-nine US cents. I also included MPCs (military payment certificates) valued at between five and fifty cents. Americans used these to slow down the black market for American money and to protect the gold flow. An American Legion Post in Missouri sent some books and several of us enjoyed *Exodus* and agreed that Leon Uris was a great storyteller.

The next day we boarded the trucks again, on our way to a search and destroy mission. We passed a couple of ARVN soldiers working on the side of the road. They were running a large grader as they leveled a new stretch of road that appeared to lead away from the paved road we were using, probably connecting a South Vietnamese army camp to the main road.

As we moved farther along the road, we saw a young Vietnamese girl directing two large water buffalo along a wide ditch that ran parallel to the road, possibly heading to her family's farm. These water buffalo were valuable to the farmers. They served as animal "tractors" that pulled plows and hauled heavy carts. They didn't require expensive petroleum fuels and subsisted on the grasses that grew in abundance in this moist climate.

We finally reached our destination and learned that we were to be a blocking force for two other US units sweeping toward our position. We advanced about a thousand meters and set up a defensive line along the edge of a rice paddy, then settled in for a long day. I had my camera with me and once we were set up, I took several shots of the rice paddy at low tide, when all of the rice plants were exposed. The view in front of me was a vast sea of thick clumps of mud, with small green shoots rising ten to fifteen inches above the mud. The plants had plenty of space between them, perhaps twelve inches. The field did not look that promising, but I had not seen rice grown before, so I trusted that the farmers who worked these fields for most of their lives knew what they were doing.

It was a clear sunny day, and we opened our C-rations around noon and ate lunch. We heard periodic reports that the other two units were continuing to advance toward our position but so far had no enemy contact.

I took a few more pictures of the field. The water had been gradually rising, and we hardly noticed the slow and imperceptible change in the water level. The rice paddy was now covered with water, and only a few inches of the grassy stalks sticking above the waterline were visible. When I looked at the pictures later, I was amazed at the dramatic difference in the look of the fields. As the tidal flows from the South China Sea caused the nearby rivers to rise and fall, water filled the rice paddies and drained them twice a day for the rest of the growing season. We would return to these rice fields or similar fields in several months and be amazed at the transition once again. The fields would be drained, and tall stalks of golden grasses would be tipped with rice grains ready to be harvested.

The RTO (radio-telephone operator) and another
soldier pause for a break while on patrol.

These scenes were repeated throughout large areas of this country, which was why Vietnam was referred to as the "Big Rice Paddy." Around 16:00 we received word that the units sweeping toward us had failed to make contact. Our job was done. We left the tranquil rice paddy and headed to our pickup point.

In the evening of the following day, we set out to prepare a nighttime ambush position. On the way to the site, we saw three unarmed men running across a field away from us. The point man ordered them to halt, but they kept running. He fired a couple of shots up in the air, but they still kept running. Five men in the front of the file opened fire. By this time the men were nearly out of range. The point man ran after them and captured one but the other two got away. MPs arrived and took the captive away for questioning. About an hour later we saw a medevac chopper land nearby. It picked up two men from the nearby ARVN compound who had been shot in the legs. We heard these three had been off post for a little "short-time" and didn't want to get caught. C'est la guerre!

Later that week we headed out on another patrol. Trucks picked us up at the water plant and drove about forty-five minutes to a road near a village. They dropped us off, and we started moving through rice paddies and elephant grass near some small rivers. The platoon sergeant told me that I would be the point man for the first couple of hours of the day. I had mixed feelings about this assignment. On the one hand, it was a vote of confidence that the "new guy" could move quietly and would be able to identify signs of enemy movement as well as any booby traps that might be in our path. On the other hand, I would be the first person that the enemy saw and would be their closest target. I moved to the front of the column where the platoon sergeant showed me a map and gave me the general direction of our route. He pointed out a taller palm tree about five hundred meters ahead of us and said to use that as an interim point of reference.

I moved cautiously forward. There was a long file of men behind me and two smaller groups about a hundred meters on the right and left flanks, but farther back. I remembered all of the training I had received and looked for signs of activity ahead: a glint of metal in the sun, some trampled grass, a string or wire stretched on the ground or between two palm trees. I also listened for voices or the sound of anything moving through the grass, shrubs, or trees ahead of us. I was wary and wanted to do this right, both for my sake as well as the safety of the men behind me.

After moving for half an hour, the platoon sergeant passed the word up to me to halt. We all knelt or squatted where we were as he came forward. He asked if I had seen anything, and I responded no. He explained that I was doing a good job of being cautious, while observing the terrain ahead and to our sides, but he would like the platoon to move a little faster so that we would reach our destination and pickup point on time by the end of the day. I agreed to move faster.

We resumed the patrol, and I moved a bit more quickly. I was still concerned about what might lie in front of me, but my confidence was growing, because we'd already covered some ground without any incident. Gradually, I picked up the pace even more until we came to a small river crossing where I stopped. It was only ten feet wide and two or three feet deep, easy to cross without a rope, but it was a vulnerable spot. Two other men came up on my flanks, and together we surveyed the land on the other side. We saw the usual palm trees and brush that grow thicker along the water's edge, but did not see any footprints or signs of any recent activity. I crossed through the muddy river. The other two followed me across; then each man moved about fifty meters away from my line of travel. I signaled to the file behind me, and they started to cross as I moved forward. In a few minutes, the entire platoon had crossed the water, and we were now moving through tall elephant grass.

The elephant grass had its own special irritants. It was only about four feet tall in this area, but it limited visibility as we looked forward. Anything or anyone could be waiting in front of us or on our flanks.

The tall grass also slowed the breeze, so this warm day got hotter as the temperature seemed to jump fifteen degrees. The platoon sergeant called for a halt, and everyone took a few sips from their canteens. I waited a few minutes, then got the word to continue moving forward. It was now past noon, and as we moved along a berm that was next to another small river, we got the order to halt and take some time to eat. I then got the order to move back to the middle of the file, and another soldier moved forward to take over point.

I felt a sense of relief and pride. Relief that I could now move to a less dangerous position and pride that I was able to lead the file for half a day without anyone getting hurt. In the back of my mind, I understood that it was just dumb luck that we did not make any enemy contact that morning. I knew that if I did this often enough, I would eventually have an unlucky day and could not predict the outcome. I walked point many more times before I had the opportunity to leave this combat zone. I never volunteered for this position, but did it to the best of my ability when assigned to the job. Some of the men took the position with eagerness, wanting to be the first to find the enemy. Most did not. Perhaps I felt that I had too much to lose. I was a year or two older than most of the men in my platoon, and I had a college degree. I believed that I had my whole life ahead of me and the potential to succeed when I returned to civilian life. I did not want to lose my life while crossing a river or walking through elephant grass.

Battalion would not be happy with our progress on that day. They would have preferred that we had successful contact with the Viet Cong on every mission, to increase the enemy body count. It was well understood by this time in the war that we were not trying to take and hold ground or villages or provinces. Our success was being measured by higher fatalities. That was the purpose of the search and destroy missions. In the meantime, I was trying to get through each mission in one piece. That day turned out to be a good day. I was still alive when we returned to our camp.

# CHAPTER 5

# CONVOY IS AMBUSHED

The next day we swept through two rather large and long villages, which took the entire day. We usually had a chance to stop and rest briefly every hour or two when on a patrol, but that day we kept going from hootch to hootch.

Between the two villages on a stretch of land was a large brick building that appeared to be a junior high school. In the center there was a courtyard where students had gathered, and three priests were saying mass. It was pleasant and surprising to hear Gregorian chant being sung by Vietnamese. Nearby was a modern statue of the Madonna and child. The entire scene was beautiful and inspiring. I was sorry I didn't have my camera with me.

We continued with the patrol, although we failed to discover any signs of enemy activity other than two oddly shaped helmets, which we forwarded to battalion.

We returned to camp to clean up, eat, and get some rest. At 01:00 the platoon sergeant woke everyone and announced we would be moving out to help another unit that was in trouble. It was raining hard as we grabbed our gear and got on trucks led by tanks from our base camp. For half an hour we sat on top of tanks, trucks and armored personnel carriers ready to go. We left the water plant and headed down the road. After a short distance, we stopped and waited again for almost an hour.

Everyone was tense, nervous, and uneasy about the impending battle. It was dark and pouring rain. It would be hard to see the enemy and hard to see the unit we were supporting. Muddy footing would make it even more difficult to maneuver in the dark. It was the first action supported by tanks, so we knew that this would be a serious conflict.

Two convoys had been ambushed a half mile down the road; one convoy was going north, and the other was going south. The VC had tried to hit both convoys as they passed, but their timing was off. Because of the distance that the vehicles kept from one another the VC only destroyed one jeep and partially wrecked a couple of small trucks. Immediately after the ambush was sprung, helicopter gunships and artillery started pounding the area and continued pounding it for several hours.

The waiting made the situation even worse. The army is famous for the practice of "hurry up and wait," but tonight was worse than usual because of the miserable rain, the need to get to the battle quickly, and our frustration at having to sit in the trucks and do nothing. There was an initial adrenaline rush as we grabbed our weapons and ammo and ran to the vehicles. We were primed for action, but there was no action, just an interminable wait in the cold, wet rain. Finally, word came down that the firefight was over; the enemy had broken off the contact. The unit that was involved had several wounded men taken to a field hospital, and the unit required no further assistance. The engines started up on the tanks and trucks, and our convoy turned around and returned to the water plant. We were ordered back to our platoon area and placed on standby alert. We could sleep as long as we kept our boots and gear on. They did not call us.

The event stirred conflicting emotions. We were glad that the unit in the ambush was safe and that we did not have to undertake a dangerous support action in dark and rainy conditions. At the same time, we had regrets about missing the chance to finally engage with an enemy that skillfully and repeatedly eluded us. It is the nature of guerilla warfare. We were the superior force, with greater manpower, training, weapons, and technology. In spite of this, they increasingly appeared to be the ones dictating the time and place of each contact. This scenario played out for the rest of my year in Vietnam.

As with most ambushes of this nature, the VC were gone five minutes after they set it off. Another company swept the area the next morning and found only two bodies. The VC, like the Americans, preferred to take their dead and wounded with them. We most likely killed and wounded one or two more. Now I understood how statisticians came up with the figure of American expenditures of $16,000 in ammunition for each VC killed.

I made a new discovery about why this war was so frustrating and why the people were not wholeheartedly behind it. On the recent patrol, when we spent the day checking out two villages, I had two pockets full of chocolate bars for the kids. Each time we checked out a hootch, I would give each of the kids a candy bar to make them smile and to make up for the intrusion. I had thought we were making progress as far as Vietnamese-American relations were concerned. The people understood that we had to check their homes. We did it quickly and efficiently and moved out, and the kids received some free candy. What more could one ask for? Well, as I found out the next day, a lot more!

I learned that the village leaders had contacted our battalion commander. While our company was searching the village, they alleged that a couple of bad apples were also picking up some odds and ends. There was over $1,000 in cash stolen, a dozen or so transistor radios ranging in value from three to fifty dollars, and numerous other items. While I naïvely thought that we were making some friends, a few "buddies" were robbing the villagers. No wonder many of these people were hard-core VC or VC sympathizers. The villages were checked every couple of months. From what I had heard, the government troops (ARVNs) were worse than the Americans with regard to pilfering when they searched villages.

There was a ten-year prison sentence in a military jail for looting, but it was so widespread and difficult to prove that the law was nothing more than a paper tiger. If the VC had the sense to refrain from senseless terrorist attacks on these villages, the United States and the government of Vietnam could never win this country, no matter how much money and military assistance was poured in. As a matter of fact, with the exception of Saigon, the VC did not make terrorist attacks on the villages in this area, which was why many of these villages were pro-Viet Cong. It was a frustrating situation to which I could see no end.

We went out on a long patrol that was mostly on hard ground for a change, a large flat area covered with small bushes and shrubs. It was easier walking, but we went farther than usual, about ten "klicks" or six miles. (A klick is equal to one kilometer or a thousand meters).

A funny incident occurred that day. Quite suddenly someone saw a person move in front of us, and we ordered him to approach us, saying, "La dai," the equivalent of "Hey, you, come over here." The guy dropped to the ground, and we started moving up on him. We didn't know if he had a larger unit behind him or how heavily armed he was, so we were cautious. I was on the left flank, so I started maneuvering to the left to block his escape and to check the edge of the area for any other VC. The point man called out to the

VC suspect a couple more times and then got ready to start spraying the area with his M-16. The suspect stood up and put his hands in the air, and we closed in on him. As we closed in, we noticed a girl on the ground pulling her pajama-like pants on and buttoning her blouse. The guy was about eighteen, and the girl was about seventeen. Embarrassment and red faces prevailed. The Vietnamese complained about American harassment, and I'm afraid I'd have to agree with them on this one. I wondered if there was something in the Geneva Convention that covered this situation.

We learned that one of the other companies got hit while on a river patrol and had contact with thirty VC. They killed a couple, and the rest got away. We had no casualties. One unusual aspect of this contact was the fact that the VC were shooting at the helicopter gunships. The VC usually hid from the gunships, because they were more heavily armed than the transport helicopters, and the VC didn't want to attract their attention. Gunships were Huey helicopters that were primarily designed to attack a position on the ground rather than serve as a transport craft. These gunships were armed with M-60 machine guns, M-134 miniguns, rockets, and in some cases, missiles. The VC had managed to shoot up four helicopters that morning about fifteen miles north of our location near the village of Phu-Li as the choppers were landing a company of troops in a field. Nobody was hurt, but the choppers suffered a few holes.

It's worth mentioning that, surprisingly, with all of this shooting, there was so little damage. It was actually very difficult to shoot a man, since he was either moving (and moving fast) or hiding behind some type of cover such as a tree or a ditch. This was true for both the VC and the Americans. As far as helicopters go, they can withstand a lot of holes before they fall out of the sky. The pilots sit in armored seats that protect them with steel plates mounted behind, under, and on the sides of the seats.

Regarding female companionship in Vietnam, there was a beverage in Saigon called "Saigon tea," a shot glass of tea priced at two dollars. It was the only thing that the bar girls would drink. To engage one of these girls in conversation, one had to keep buying her Saigon tea, which could get very expensive. These girls were usually better looking than the girls in the smaller villages and towns. It could cost anywhere from forty to eighty dollars for a couple of hours of conversation! One guy in our company spent sixty-eight dollars on Saigon tea conversation and never slept with the girl. The girls in Saigon charged from fifteen to fifty dollars for "short-time" and more for a whole night's companionship.

We were located in an area best described as a suburb of Saigon. There were small villages or hamlets every two miles in every direction. This water plant was located on one of the biggest four-lane highways in the country. The highway extended north from Saigon, so it was always busy during the day with military vehicles, bicycles, scooters, motorcycles, and Lambrettas.

Our platoon went out on a new patrol through dry land, through three villages that had been abandoned, burned out, or bombed by us, the VC, or both. There was one lone sniper who spent most of the day firing at us. He'd fire one shot, and everybody would hit the dirt. We'd wait for a second shot, but none would come. After ten minutes or so, we'd get up and move out. Half an hour later he'd fire one more shot, and the whole process would be repeated. He continued firing at us throughout the day without hitting anyone.

We didn't try to catch him, because we assumed that he was trying to bait us into an ambush.

We had one of our busiest days on Friday, August 30, when we went out on three different patrols via helicopter. That was four rides in one day. These patrols were standard search and destroy missions. We spent an average of two hours moving through each location and failed to uncover any evidence of recent VC activity. We suspected that Intelligence had some bad information, or we were supposed to be rechecking areas that had been overlooked on recent patrols by other units. In any event, it kept us and the chopper pilots busy all day.

We were not familiar with the names of the helicopter units that ferried us around, but we grew to recognize the symbols they painted on their aircraft. During this time, most of the choppers had a white tomahawk painted on the nose of the chopper or on the pilot's door. We later learned that they were from the 128th Assault Helicopter Company, also known as the "Tomahawks."

Christina sent me a letter describing a marine who'd returned from Vietnam recently. He had been with a unit up north that had run short of drinking water, so they had started drinking beer that had been stashed in the camp. Unfortunately, I was not that lucky, since I was stationed at a water plant that processed millions of gallons of water.

One problem was the shortage of clean socks. We'd run out of socks every week or so due to the wet and muddy patrols. I learned to hoard several pairs of socks and wash them by hand. When supply ran short, I'd start using my personal inventory.

I sent another letter to my younger brother, Gary, and enclosed two US one-dollar bills. "These are two examples of what is commonly known as the greenback. It is valued at one hundred cents to the dollar. It is very highly thought of over here. As a matter of fact, it is so highly thought of that I could get ten years in a military prison if I get caught with this money, which is the reason I am sending it to you! I received the money yesterday along with some black-and-white prints that I had left in San Francisco for developing. I gave the owner a three-dollar deposit and my old address. The pictures only cost a dollar, and he sent me the change. The package has been bouncing around in military post offices for the last month and a half, which is why I just received it yesterday."

We went out on another patrol and found a VC hospital bunker system by a river. There was a wide variety of supplies including penicillin, vitamins, and bandages. The VC were big on vitamin C and used it as a cure-all. Shotgun wound in the leg? Have plenty of vitamin C, and you'll be OK, according to their theories.

Our platoon had a stand-down the next day, but I was on a detail, filling sandbags. It wasn't too bad, since it was my turn anyway, and we managed to get some help with the job. The sergeant grabbed three cases of C-rations, and we rode in a truck along Highway 316 a short distance from the water plant to a group of Vietnamese, who were willing to work as day laborers. There were about nine people, a mix of men and women. The sergeant offered them two cases of C-rations as compensation for filling sandbags, and they quickly agreed.

We provided several stacks of sandbags and large shovels, and they eagerly started filling the bags. The soil at this location was loose and easy to handle. As they finished filling the sandbags, we loaded them on the truck. We were generally aware that rice and rubber were two of the major crops in Vietnam, but we were also convinced that sandbags were a major product of the country. The total bags filled by soldiers and civilians during the entire length of the conflict must have been in the millions. They were used to protect barracks, bunkers, mortar and artillery positions, gate entrances, and mess halls. Every soldier in Vietnam spent a significant part of his tour filling, moving, or directing the movement of sandbags.

During this detail we were positioned on a busy road, where there was a steady flow of vehicles of all types and sizes. They were driven by soldiers from South Vietnam and the United States as well as civilians on their way to or from Saigon. We also realized that our presence on the side of the road was noted by some entrepreneurial individuals. Within half an hour of our arrival, half a dozen vendors showed up and offered to sell us cold sodas and beer from Styrofoam coolers packed with ice. The beverage containers were sealed, so they were generally safe to drink. Most soldiers purchased a couple of sodas, while a few grabbed a single beer. We were technically on a mission and wanted to remain alert enough to defend ourselves if we perceived a threat. The area turned out to be relatively safe in the daytime, and we were more relaxed than we would be in the boonies.

We opened a case of C-rations for lunch, ate what we needed, and shared the rest with the workers who took a break for lunch. They brought their own food and saved the extra canned goods for trade or barter on the black market.

A couple of older girls showed up and started laughing with a couple of the youngest members of our squad. After a lengthy discussion, two of the guys headed away from the road with the girls and walked behind the trees near the power line. They returned a half hour later. In the meantime, the pile of sandbags increased in the truck. All of the bags were now filled, and we picked up the shovels, boarded the truck, waved good-bye to the civilians, and returned to the water plant. The change of routine for us helped to make up for some of the more difficult days. I took the opportunity to take some pictures of the crew filling the bags along with several shots of the various vehicles driving along the highway.

The following day we were back in the boonies checking rivers and riverbanks. We found five weapons and several cans of ammunition. There were three AK-47s and two M-1 carbines. The AK-47s were Russian or Czech, but the M-1s were American-made, probably purchased on the black market. It was a relatively small number of weapons but enough to supply a Viet Cong squad with the firepower needed for an ambush. We had probably helped prevent or minimize an attack on our company or some other company that operated in this area.

In early September, we had a belated Labor Day celebration during a stand-down. The festivities included a barbecue, beer, and a hi-fi set with the volume turned on high. The music was a mix of popular songs including, "People Got to Be Free," "Dance to the Music," and "Jumpin' Jack Flash." I had a couple of beers and was feeling pretty good. Everyone was happy to have a reason to celebrate.

That night I was assigned to a special guard detail with seven other men. Our job was to protect a barge containing military cargo in the middle of a wide river. We rode on tanks and armored personnel carriers to a bridge near the barge. Our vehicles were in a convoy with a tank in the lead. The convoy was supposed to cross the bridge, turn around, and drop us off. We crossed the bridge without incident, and the tank turned around. Suddenly an old truck being driven by a South Vietnamese man came speeding past us on the left. The rules of the road required that you pass a convoy on the right only, and you never pass on a bridge. I was on the third vehicle and saw this truck slam on its brakes as it sought to avoid a head-on collision with the lead tank, which had turned around and was now heading back across the bridge. The tank driver was so annoyed that he started moving forward toward the truck. The driver, seeing a forty-ton tank bearing down on him, threw the truck into reverse and backed it halfway across the bridge until he could finally get into the other lane. It was similar to two bulls with horns challenging each other, only in this case, one was much bigger than the other.

We walked down to the base of the bridge and boarded PBRs, fast boats that took us to the barge a mile down the river. These boats really moved. We seemed to be going about thirty miles an hour, with spray flying from the boat. We finally reached the barge, which was anchored in the middle of a river that was a half-mile wide at this point. We took turns staying awake on guard duty while the others played cards, went swimming, or slept. The swimming was a bit dangerous, but we took some chances. We'd dive off the upstream end and swim toward the downstream end of the barge, careful not to get carried away by the current. The danger was that we'd likely get shot by our own troops if we tried to get to the shore. At night, they'd shoot anything that moved in the water. We climbed back on the barge, quieted down, and spent the night without incident.

A few days later, we had some bad luck on another patrol. The company was conducting a sweep along a river, and our platoon was checking the banks when someone in one of the other platoons set off a booby trap. It was a Chinese-made grenade with a wire tied to a tree. Two guys were hit with shrapnel and were flown out on a medevac in about ten minutes. At the same time we started receiving fire from the VC. The other platoon started firing a grenade launcher at the VC position, which was firing an AK-47 at us. One of the grenades from the launcher hit a tree or a branch and exploded close to our position, wounding one of our men. He was also dusted off in about ten minutes. By this time, the VC had disappeared. None of the three men who were flown out were seriously wounded, and they were back in the field in three or four weeks.

This guerilla warfare was starting to fall into a familiar pattern. We'd surprise them with a patrol or an ambush, then they'd surprise us with an ambush or a booby trap. Firefights lasted a very short time. Casualties generally moved in tandem for both sides. It seemed to be a long-term process of attrition. They would have a few wounded with one or two men killed, and we would have a few wounded with one or none killed. There were very few set battles in our area of operation. I'd only been there for three months, and the future for our overall mission did not look promising. I made a personal resolution to be extra careful each day. I wanted to complete my tour and get the hell out of there.

We were checking rivers again, and I brought my new camera with me and left it with a buddy who was in a boat. I retrieved it briefly to get a couple of pictures and started heading back to the boat. To be safe, I placed the camera on an air mattress and gently pushed the mattress along toward the boat. As I was paddling, a big gust of wind came along and flipped the mattress over. The camera got wet, but I caught it quickly and tossed it into the boat. This time I planned to send it to the manufacturer in Japan to have it repaired.

We completed the river portion of our patrol, and the boats dropped us off at a new position, where we continued to patrol on land. In the middle of the afternoon, one of the radiomen in our platoon stepped on a booby trap and was seriously hurt when it exploded. He had shrapnel in his back and legs. He was evacuated on a medevac chopper, and it was a while before he returned to our unit.

Christina sent me a news clipping. I told her that I read the article describing the riot on August 29 in Long Binh Jail (this is the Camp LBJ that I mentioned earlier). It was the military jail for soldiers charged with serious offenses. My hootchmate knew a guy who had just gotten out of LBJ a few days earlier. He said it was a race riot. One man was killed by the mob that was rioting.

We checked out more rivers the next day and found nothing. At one point someone thought that they saw VC in a field, and they called in heavy artillery and jets to pound the area. We dropped very low to the ground and hugged the earth to avoid any stray shrapnel from these combined strikes. When it was all over we looked for signs of movement in the area but didn't see anything. Then we formed up in an assault line and slowly swept through the field. We failed to find any weapons, wounded VC, or even blood trails that might indicate that an enemy had been there. It probably made sense to bring in bigger firepower to be certain, but the only certain thing that day was that the taxpayers got a big bill for some very expensive ordnance.

The next day was a fairly good day, even though it rained the whole time that we were out in the field. We had no contact. The rain continued all night long. When we finally returned to the water plant, we spent the evening packing our gear. We had learned that we were moving to a new base camp in the morning. I had grown accustomed to life here. My hootch wasn't luxurious by any means, but it had been "home" for two months. The presence of the tank and the artillery units made it feel a bit more secure. I also knew that I would miss the showers with a seemingly endless supply of water. I wondered what our new camp would be like.

# CHAPTER 6

# NDP—LIVING IN THE BOONIES

On Thursday, September 12, we made the move from the water plant to a new NDP (night defensive position) in the boonies. Our men and our gear were shuttled in with helicopters, because there were no passable roads near this camp. It was a long day as we unloaded our gear and weapons, found our new hootches, and started to get familiar with our new surroundings. I spent the rest of that day filling sandbags and was tired. I had also been assigned guard duty in the tower from 04:00 to 06:00 the next morning.

The second day at our new camp found us all exhausted. Our unit had more men than the previous unit that had left this camp, so we were encouraged to build additional hootches. The army thoughtfully provided plenty of sandbags, so we started working on new housing. We helped each other to fill enough sandbags to get the walls up to a height of at least four feet. Then the new tenants finished off the hootches with sheets of plastic, metal stakes and plywood for the roof and more sandbags. The new homes were two sandbags thick, with a wooden-door-type window. The design made them dry and cooler during the day, and safer from stray rounds that might come our way.

This new base camp was on dry ground in the middle of a big clearing surrounded by rice paddies and mud. It was about five hundred meters in diameter and roughly the shape of a circle. There were three sets of barbed concertina wire surrounding the camp. The wood line (palm trees and bushes) was about a thousand meters away from the perimeter. If anyone tried to hit the camp, they would have to crawl five hundred meters on flat land in the open before they could even get in range to start firing. This camp had never been hit before.

At this time the three other infantry platoons were going out on search and destroy missions as well as night ambushes. My platoon was not going out on patrols, but was operating like a mortar platoon, taking care of our three guns, and firing at night in areas of suspected enemy targets with no specific target in sight. A few nights after our arrival, a South Vietnamese company sprang an ambush on some VC. We supported them by firing illumination rounds for an hour.

The illumination round goes up in the air and explodes, releasing a flare attached to a parachute that lights up an area of a thousand meters by a thousand meters. The parachute floats slowly to the ground, providing illumination for sixty seconds, which is plenty of time to locate enemy positions. Rounds can be fired sequentially to provide almost continuous lighting of the battlefield.

In addition to the regular perimeter guards and lookout posts, there was a wooden guard tower equipped with a radar set designed for picking up movement around our perimeter. One man from each of the four platoons was selected to operate the radar set, including me. I received training on the set and was then able to pick up the movement of water buffalo (there were several in the area) and the movement of men. It was another week before I became good at it. My shift was from 04:00 to 06:00 every morning. The upside of manning the radar device was that I didn't have to go outside the wire at night on four-man listening posts or on night ambushes.

Our camp was equipped with a primitive but effective shower consisting of a tripod of metal engineer stakes joined together at the top point about eight feet off the ground. A canvas bag was fastened to the top, with a shower head about five inches in diameter at the bottom of the bag. The shower station included a small wooden floor made from an ammo crate and was protected by a seven-foot-high stack of wooden ammo crates that were filled with dirt.

We'd walk over to the water tank trailer and fill a two-gallon container with water. We'd then fill the canvas bag and quickly shower while the water flowed down. After drying off, we'd go back to our hootch and get into a dry set of fatigues. Even if there were no dry fatigues, I'd usually find a clean pair of socks that I had carefully saved so that my feet would stay dry.

In the morning, we'd grab a small plastic pan or our metal helmet and fill it at the water trailer. We used shaving cream and a razor to shave while looking in a small personal mirror we kept with our gear. It was satisfying to clean up, even if we only stayed clean for a short time.

Since the NDP was located in the boonies with no road access, all of our supplies: food, water, and ammo were delivered by helicopter, the large, twin-rotor Chinook helicopters that looked like oversized buses and were about three times as long.

They arrived every two or three days, but more frequently if we used ammunition (for rifles and mortars) at a faster rate due to combat activity. When the Chinook was inbound, the supply specialist headed out to the landing zone inside our wire and popped a colored smoke grenade. The chopper pilot identified the color of the smoke and headed in for a landing.

Earlier in the war, chopper pilots would simply acknowledge that they had seen a smoke grenade and fly into the spot where the smoke appeared. The Viet Cong started to pop captured US smoke grenades in nearby fields, and hapless pilots would land in these fields and be subjected to intense small arms fire. After several choppers were shot down, the procedure was changed.

As the chopper approached, we'd see three elements of the delivery. The chopper itself was on top, with a water tank trailer suspended from a large hook under the belly of the chopper. Suspended from the bottom of the water trailer was a large cargo net filled with cases of food and ammo.

The Chinook slowly lowered itself to the ground until the cargo net lay flat, then moved forward slightly so the water trailer could reach the ground without crushing the contents of the cargo net. The final step was the most dangerous part of the delivery as the supply specialist climbed on top of the water trailer and slipped the connecting strap from the trailer out of the hook at the bottom of the chopper. Once this step was completed, the chopper pilot maneuvered the craft forward about 150 feet and lowered it to the ground. The crew chief lowered the rear ramp, and any personnel who were coming in to our camp walked down the ramp.

The procedure was reversed when the Chinook took off. A separate cargo net filled with laundry and other items was attached to an empty water trailer. Outbound personnel would run up the rear ramp of the chopper. When the chopper started to rise, it would hover about fifteen feet off the ground while the supply specialist stood on top of the water trailer and attached it to the hook hanging from the Chinook. Once connected, he jumped from the trailer and ran a short distance as the pilot slowly moved up into the air.

I witnessed this delicate ballet more than two dozen times and always marveled at the successful outcome. The contrast between the weight of the thirty-three-thousand-pound helicopter and the 150-pound man underneath was like an elephant trying to sit on a small dog that jumps out of the way just as the elephant touches the ground.

The movement of the supplies inside the camp was another choreographed maneuver. Every available soldier was called to the cargo net as the ammo boxes were handed off. The first soldier would grab the rope handle on the front side of the first ammo box. The next soldier would grab the rear handle of the first box with one hand and the front handle of the next box with the other hand. When all of the ammo boxes were lifted off the ground, the conga line moved toward the mortar pits where the ammo boxes were neatly stacked. They'd turn around, go back to the cargo net, and grab a case of C-rations, which they'd carry to the mess tent. The entire cycle from the landing of the Chinook to the neat stacking of C-rations at the mess tent took less than twenty minutes.

A soldier prepares to attach an empty water trailer to the hook under the belly of the Chinook that keeps the NDP supplied with food, water, and ammunition.

The Chaplain celebrates
Mass on one of his visits.

A scout dog and his handler
get ready to move.

My fiancée sent me a letter mentioning that she purchased her first car, a yellow Opel with a stick shift! She needed the car to visit families for her new job as a caseworker with an adoption agency. We had discussed the types of cars she was considering in a series of letters to each other. I missed being there to share the experience with her but knew that we both had to focus on our own lives for the time being.

Every few weeks a chaplain would visit our camp, but we often missed the visit if we happened to be out in the field when he showed up. If the chaplain was a priest, he would set up a basic altar on a table or on the side of a jeep, don a simple robe, and say mass for the Catholic men. He would also invite others to attend a shorter session for a generic prayer and a quick blessing.

Everyone was respectful of the chaplains regardless of their declared faith, even though some claimed to be atheists or agnostics.

It was an opportunity to briefly connect with a ritual that seemed familiar and reminded men of home.

By this time we all knew someone who had been killed or wounded. Death was a definite possibility out on patrol or even sitting in the camp eating a meal while perched on a sandbag. We had heard the phrase "there are no atheists in foxholes," and its meaning seemed much more relevant and personal in our current situation.

We received a new load of mortar shells from the Chinook resupply chopper and spent the morning unpacking them. We cut the protective outer padding and paper with a knife to reach the black corrugated canisters. Then we'd twist off the cap at the end of the canister and pull out the mortar round. The next step was to remove the black tape and plastic at the bottom of the round that covered the small cloth powder charges and check the fuse. The mortar round was then placed back in the black canister ready for use when needed. All that the gunner had to do was open the canister, pull off the correct number of powder charges to match the force needed to propel the round, and finally, drop the round into the mortar tube. When the round hit the bottom of the tube, it hit a firing pin that ignited a basic charge and also ignited any powder bags attached to the round. The heated gases quickly expanded and forced the round to fly out of the tube on its planned trajectory. The azimuth (direction) and elevation of the mortar tube had been previously set based on instructions from the FDC (fire direction center).

After the mortar rounds were checked and stored, we had some free time. Someone brought out a set of darts and set up a target at the back of a hootch. Most members of the platoon took turns with the darts. The target was riddled with irony as well as holes from the darts. It was a recruiting poster that depicted a group of clean-cut ROTC students sitting at desks wearing their Class A green uniforms and taking notes while the instructor covered some element of military history.

The headline read ENROLL IN THE ARMY. The irony lay in the fact that the majority of soldiers in our company were draftees who would rather not be in Vietnam. Most of the others were enlistees who, feeling that the draft was inevitable, enlisted so they could choose a field of training or simply get their military service over with and move on with their lives. If this were a dart board in a stateside bar, the winner would get a free pitcher of beer. Here, it was a pat on the back and bragging rights for a couple of days.

In another hootch, a card game was underway. Poker was the preferred game, using poker chips purchased with military payment certificates, a substitute for greenbacks. There was a regular cadre of five or six players who would start a game with as little as an hour of free time available. As a result, there was a game going on most evenings and stand-down days when we had the opportunity to play. Other members of the platoon were welcome to join the game when someone dropped out. The general rule was dealer's choice, and since the soldiers hailed from cities and towns all over the United States there were endless variations and permutations of poker games introduced over the course of a year.

When the platoon went out on patrols or ambushes for four or five days in a row, there would be a hiatus for a few days. Exhaustion set in, and sleep became more valuable than a poker game.

Even though it was monsoon season, it turned out to be one of the hottest and driest in years. The ground was turning into dust that created small dust storms when the helicopters landed.

We received some more bad news on Saturday, September 14. General Ware, commander of the 1st Infantry Division, was killed in a helicopter crash. Our division would be getting a new general. We wondered if he would initiate any new policies that would affect us.

Monsoon rains pour down most days.

Poker games provide a
respite in the field.

Mortar crews remove packing materials from the rounds,
so they are ready to fire when needed.

A few nights later, eight of us went out on a detail to set up a booby trap across a nearby river by stringing up a fine wire about a foot above the water. The wire was connected to a battery and explosives. A sampan going down the river at night would hit the wire and set off the explosives. We had just finished setting it up when the platoon sergeant said he thought he saw something move on the other bank. He opened up, and we all started firing. I fired almost forty rounds before we stopped. While we were firing, the explosives went off with a loud bang. We then called in mortar fire from the rest of the platoon, which was back in our camp. When the mortar fire ended, we checked out the other bank and the area behind it but failed to find any VC. We returned to the NDP.

The whole exercise took less than two hours. The platoon sergeant claimed the explosives went off because someone was moving on the other bank, but I strongly suspected that a round hit the wire or shook the dirt on the other bank where it was attached. We repeated this booby trap exercise every evening. Most nights were pretty quiet, and it would be many weeks before the wire was tripped again.

One day we didn't receive any mail, because someone got to the supply chopper pad too late to load the mail sack. They also failed to bring any ice, and all the milk they had brought in earlier turned sour. The biggest disappointment was missing the mail. We could tolerate lots of issues and all sorts of logistical problems, but not a mix-up in the mail.

There was good news that evening when the army came through for us. It was almost dark when a little two-man LOH (light observation helicopters) landed, dropped off two mail sacks, and quickly took off. They rarely landed at this camp after dark due to the risks, but they knew the importance of the mail.

After a long dry spell, it finally started raining heavily one afternoon and cooled things off quite a bit. Our mortar platoon was in camp, so we took off our clothes, grabbed bars of soap, and started taking showers in the middle of the camp. Normally, we'd have to walk out to the water trailer and carry water to the shower station.

It was Saturday, September 21, and the monsoon season had started in earnest. It rained all afternoon and most of the night for two full days. I remembered the patrols we'd had just a few weeks ago when it did rain. We would sit in the rain or walk through the rain and get thoroughly wet. I felt fortunate for the moment, since we were not going out on patrols, although this would probably change.

The rain was very intense. The inside of my hootch was pretty dry, but every once in a while, we'd have to go out and sight our mortars on possible targets, and we'd get soaked. I had two sets of fatigues that I kept switching, but now it was getting hard to keep even one pair dry.

The lieutenant in charge of our platoon had been transferred to another unit about a month and a half earlier, and the platoon sergeant had been in charge in the interim. A new lieutenant arrived. We didn't know much about him, but we wondered what changes he might make.

We finally received mosquito nets from supply. They would provide some protection from mosquitoes at night and flies when we slept during the day.

On Monday, September 23, they flew in a couple of dentists and all sorts of portable equipment including air hoses, drills, etc. They cleaned, checked, drilled, filled, and pulled teeth. I had mine cleaned, but I didn't need any work done.

Firing mortars can be hazardous, and I had a lump on the side of my head the size of a golf ball to prove it. One evening we were firing mortars, and after I'd drop each round down the tube, I'd bend to my left and cover my ears with my hands to get out of the way of the round coming out of the barrel and to keep from bursting an eardrum. As I was going down, my partner was handing me another round. I was moving toward the round as it was coming toward me, so we met in the middle. It was just a normal part of fast-moving army life, but the round clearly made an impression on me.

Two days later, two Red Cross female volunteers (Red Cross Girls) came out by helicopter with a modified version of the Risk game on a big plastic board played by two teams. My team won in about twenty minutes. When the game was over, they sat around and talked for a couple of hours. There was, however, a method in the army's madness, because an hour later, the medics had everyone get their shot records, pulled out a case of needles and serums, and started bringing everyone's shot records up to date. Luckily, I only had to get one shot, for tetanus, since it had been over a year since my last one.

An unnamed NDP in the boonies. The primary barrier against enemy attack was a ring of concertina wire surrounding the camp. Platoons went out on daytime patrols and night ambushes.

The white flash of a mortar
being fired at night.

The daily view.

Life at this camp was pretty good. We did some firing during the night, but we were able to sleep later and usually got up about 07:30 (late for the army). We cleaned our hootches and weapons and had some time to read or play cards.

There was an occasional opportunity for recreation in the field. One sunny day our mortar platoon had a stand-down. The early morning routines were completed: chow, shave, clean weapons, etc.

A baseball bat and a couple of softballs appeared. Some of the men had brought baseball gloves with them, so we had three gloves in the field while the rest used bare hands to catch balls.

The platoon split into two teams of roughly ten men each. We picked a flat area inside the wire which was normally used for helicopter landings. The field was set up with sandbags used for first, second, third, and home plate. Fortunately, it had not rained for a couple of days, so the field was dry and dusty. The game began.

Two of the squad leaders became captains and assigned field positions to their team members. The standard uniform for both teams consisted of olive-drab boxer shorts and shower sandals. Some of the men wore fatigue pants as well. It was a hot, dry day, so everyone was shirtless. The sandals did not provide much foot support when running the bases, but it was the preferred foot gear on dry days, because it allowed the feet to dry out after spending several days in wet jungle boots while crossing rivers and rice paddies.

I had played little league in Brooklyn, New York, sponsored by the Paragon Oil Distributor, but I was not an outstanding player. We wound up in last place in our league. On this day I chose to play the role of sports photographer and practice getting action shots of the players who truly loved the game. I set the shutter speed at 1/500 of a second and used a large enough f-stop opening to allow light to enter the lens in the briefest exposure time to leave an image on the film emulsion. I had captured dozens of images including a few dramatic shots of the ball setting off on a long arc just inches after being propelled by the bat. The concentrated grimace of the batters added to the drama of the photos.

It turned out to be a great game for everyone. Every player managed to hit a ball, and some even scored home runs. There were some close calls at a couple of the bases, but they somehow reached an agreement about who was safe, and who was not. The winning team cheered at the end of the game. They had captured hero status for the next couple of days.

I was amassing quite a selection of black-and-white prints detailing our daily activities. Several guys requested additional prints to keep or send home. I numbered all the prints and circulated them around the platoon for the guys to place orders at ten cents a print (my processing cost at the PX was five cents a print). The men in the platoon were very happy with the three-by-five prints, because they were crisp and clear. The net profit wasn't a lot, but it helped cover some of the costs of the two cameras I had lost and a replacement camera I picked up at the PX.

# CHAPTER 7

# NEW ASSIGNMENT—FORWARD OBSERVER

It continued to rain every day. The company went out on a sweep and hit a booby trap made with a grenade tied to a wire. One man was killed, and three were wounded. That night everyone in the company was feeling pretty low. When I first arrived in Vietnam, a sergeant had said that we hardly ever hit booby traps in this area, since most of them were set up north near Pleiku and the DMZ, where enemy activity was the heaviest. As it turned out this was bad information. In my first three months in the field, booby traps caused the death of one man and wounded a dozen more. We hadn't had so much as a cut finger due to direct enemy action. We were learning what guerilla warfare was all about.

My fiancée asked if my letters were censored, since I was specific about our location. The truth was that we were in the boonies, in the middle of nowhere, and this place had no real name. Everyone referred to the place as the "Delta NDP." Delta was the designation of our company and NDP stood for night defensive position. We were approximately eight miles northeast of Saigon, but there was nothing to mark our position other than a little cross mark on a map.

It was still raining every day, so all of our gear was pretty damp. We found some diversion from the dreariness with a popular cartoon strip called *Nguyen Charlie* that was running in the *Pacific Stars & Stripes*, a military newspaper. It was produced by cartoonist Corky Trinidad and described the daily tribulations of a Viet Cong soldier; kind of a reverse *Beetle Bailey*. It was interesting, because it put a face on an enemy that we seldom saw. I started sending copies of this cartoon strip to my family.

My new camera (the third in three months) was working well. Since it wasn't waterproof, I was still concerned about getting it wet in the field. I tried to pick the days carefully when bringing my camera along on missions, checking the maps the night before, and trying to avoid patrols with too many river crossings. I often took pictures inside our base camps and brought a camera on patrols about once every two weeks. My first priority was being alert and staying alive. I was focused on my M-16 and everything going on around me. When we stopped for a break or lunch with surrounding security for the platoon, I opened the camera case and quickly took a series of photos using black-and-white or color slide film. When I first arrived in Vietnam I initially thought that the color film and slide film they sold in the PX was very expensive, but, I learned that the price included processing. It was a pleasant surprise when I realized that I could send the film to a lab in the States, and they would ship the finished slides directly to Christina.

I was averaging four or five rolls of slides and a similar number of black-and-white rolls when I went out. I felt that this would be one of the most unique experiences of my life, and I wanted to capture as much of it on film as possible without endangering myself or others.

I started a new job. Though I was still in the mortar platoon, I was now a forward observer (FO), since the current FO was heading home. Armed with my own set of maps, a new compass, and a grease pencil, I went out with a line platoon on search and destroy missions and called in mortars or artillery fire when they needed it. I also went out on night ambushes every few days and called in illumination rounds if they spotted something. I carried my own radio so that I had direct communication with my mortar platoon as well as the artillery batteries back at Di An or the water plant.

My fiancée asked if I had volunteered for this position. The answer was yes, for a variety of reasons, primarily, because it was more interesting and required some analytic skills, which was a pleasant change.

Calling in rounds wasn't that difficult. The critical aspect of the job was reading a map accurately so that I knew exactly where I was at any given time. This was difficult during the day because the land was very flat and the fields and rice paddies all looked alike. The key to getting it right was to pinpoint the spot where we landed the choppers and to then make good estimates of the distance and direction that we were walking. There were no hills or mountains in our area of operation to use as reference points, so we sometimes relied on the location of bends and curves in some of the larger rivers when we could see them.

It was even more difficult to fix a position on a night ambush, but we were usually dropped off close to the planned ambush site and had to move only a short distance. Prior to each mission, I would sit down with the guys in the FDC (fire direction center) and locate our planned ambush site for night missions. We'd set up three or four preplanned target sites that would be three or four hundred meters around our position. In this way, if we needed quick fire support, I could call in one of these targets with a code name like Alpha 3 or Bravo 4 and the first round would land in a couple of minutes. I would then call back and adjust the location of the next round by saying left or right fifty meters or add fifty or drop a hundred meters. At this point, the mortar round would be right on top of the target, and I'd call in the order to "fire for effect." The mortar or artillery crew would then fire multiple rounds of HE (high explosives) on the enemy site.

I had been going out with the company for the previous few days along with the artillery officer. Every half hour, he asked me for locations that he'd call in to headquarters. I had been accurate for all of the calls every day, so the following day was my last day of practice map reading. I was now the official FO for my company.

My fiancée asked about the racial makeup of my platoon. The majority of the men were white. There were several African American men in my platoon and many in the company. In fact, one of my hootchmates, Ezell, was black. There were also a few Hispanic and Asian Americans. There was no apparent discrimination in our company, which was a good thing; we had to work closely together, and our lives depended on our buddies, regardless of race. Too bad this mutual respect didn't carry over back in the States. I believed that army vets would have more tolerant views on race relations than people who had never lived with members of a group that had suffered prejudice.

On October 6, there was a tragic accident. The lieutenant in charge of one of the infantry platoons planned a training exercise during one of their stand-down days. He was concerned that his men were taking too long to cross rivers while on patrol and were vulnerable to attack while in this dangerous situation. It was only scheduled to last for a couple of hours, so they would still have time to clean their gear and rest afterward.

The platoon donned their field gear and headed to a small river nearby, just beyond the tree line of our NDP. It was not a particularly wide river, perhaps fifty feet at this point, with a moderate current.

It was to be a simple exercise. The platoon stopped on one side of the river, set up security on both flanks, and carefully looked for any sign of enemy movement on the other side. There was no indication of VC in the area. One of the soldiers pulled a rope as he swam across the river. When he reached the other side, he tied his end of the rope to a strong palm tree.

The first man grabbed the rope and started to pull himself across, moving hand over hand. The rope had some slack in it, so it was underwater for a short distance in the middle of the river. A second, then a third soldier followed. One of the men panicked and let go of the rope. He was weighed down with his weapon and two cans of machine gun ammo, and he disappeared from view.

The radio operator called back to our camp and asked for some swimmers to run to the river to help the drowning man. Wearing my green boxer shorts and sandals I, along with four other soldiers, sprinted the short distance to the river and jumped in. Some of us went to the opposite bank, and the rest stayed on the near bank. We dove under the water and felt along the bottom for the missing soldier. We worked our way to the center of the river, staying near the rope where he disappeared. We were surprised at the depth of the river in the center, perhaps eight or ten feet, and the speed of the current, which was stronger than it appeared on the surface.

We didn't find him at this location, so we went back to the riverbanks, moved about five feet downriver from the rope, and repeated the procedure. We continued to dive and to search for the man with our feet, but the current was forcing us rapidly downstream making it difficult to stay in one spot. We repeated the procedure until we were almost fifty feet downstream. We returned to the rope and started diving again, staying closer to the riverbank and checking the bottom with the assumption that he might have gotten snagged on a tree root along the river's edge. We continued this process for about thirty minutes.

Battalion headquarters had received a message and sent two boats from another nearby mission. They were basic boats with a metal hull and an outboard motor, each with a grappling hook attached to a length of rope. They started near the rope stretched across the river and dragged the river with the hooks. They finally retrieved the body from the center of the river about thirty feet from the rope. The medic gave him artificial respiration on the shore, but since he had been under water for an hour and a half, he was dead. They carried the soldier's body back to our base camp.

A small observation helicopter arrived with a colonel from battalion. He looked at the body and ordered the medic to resume artificial respiration on the man. The medic was incredulous but complied with the order. There was no chance that the man could have survived. In spite of this, the medic continued artificial respiration until the colonel told him to stop. A medevac chopper arrived and took the man's body away.

We were all very upset about this incident. We could understand being shot or wounded in a firefight. We could even accept dying from a wound from a booby trap. These were the risks we took every day. But this was even worse than a booby trap, because it had nothing to do with the enemy. It wasn't really a case of incompetence, because we had made river crossings with slack ropes before and always had our full complement of gear on. We could not understand dying from an incident like this. It was a tragedy that was hard to explain.

We were also deeply disturbed that the colonel forced the medic to continue working on a dead body when there was no conceivable way that he could have been revived. The colonel wanted to make sure he could state in his report that everything had been done to save the man. The medic, who had seen this behavior before, was visibly troubled but kept his mouth shut.

The lieutenant who set up the exercise was distraught. It was not an unusually risky exercise. There was no rush to complete it in an unreasonably short period of time. It was the worst fatality that I had witnessed since arriving in Vietnam. It would not be the last.

I received some good news in the mail. The camera manufacturer in Japan believed that my waterlogged camera could be repaired! As soon as it was returned, I would have two cameras: one for slide film and the other for black-and-white film. With only one camera, I was missing sunsets when using black-and-white film and shots of interest only to the men in the platoon when using slide film.

A couple of nights later, I went out on my first ambush mission as FO. The twenty-five-pound radio (PRC-25) was attached to my backpack frame as I headed out on foot through the wire of our base camp. We left around 18:00 and moved through the fields and palm trees for about an hour and a half until we reached the ambush site. It was at the edge of a river where VC activity was recently reported. We set up in an L-shaped ambush. The long part of the L was made up of a line of troops spread out along the riverbank facing the river and the opposite bank. The short part of the L was comprised of a line of troops at the left end of the river facing forward in our direction of travel. We felt reasonably secure from our rear section, since we had just moved from that area without detecting any VC. There was a long open field to the left of our direction of travel that allowed us early warning if the Viet Cong were to advance from that side.

To prepare for the long night ahead, we found an elevated dry spot that provided good visibility across the river. Paired with another soldier, I stationed myself in the center on the riverbank. We would share two-hour shifts on and off, watching throughout the night. It was a long night, and I found it hard to sleep. Every little sound of an animal or an odd ripple of the current caused me to focus on that spot. The partial moon provided enough light to see the outline of palms and bushes on the other side of the river as well as the glints of light on the river's surface that would quickly reveal the movement of a boat or people in the water. I was equipped with a radio, so I received periodic calls throughout the night from headquarters. The barely audible voice came over the receiver, "Delta 2, provide sit-rep (situation report), click twice for OK." I responded by squeezing the transmit button on the handset twice. Speaking into the handset would have created noise and attracted attention. There was no sound at my position. By squeezing the transmit button, the headquarters receiver heard a squawk-squawk sound like a brief element of static. The barely audible voice at headquarters acknowledged with a brief "Affirmative Delta 2, understand OK." and went on to call another position at some other ambush site in the operating area.

When dawn finally arrived, we gathered our gear and headed back to our camp. No enemy contact that night, but we were in place and ready for anything. Ambush missions were a lot like the old game Battleship. You picked a spot on a grid and waited to see if something happened when you got there. Nothing happened that day, but most of us were not disappointed. It was one more day behind us.

The next night we were back in camp manning the mortars. We completed a live fire mission. Some ARVNs blew an ambush they had set up about five hundred meters from where we were positioned the previous night. We fired illumination rounds over the area to expose the enemy. We also fired HE (high-explosive) rounds. I did not know the outcome of the ambush, but no medevac choppers headed in their direction, so I assumed they were all right. As an FO, I normally didn't fire the mortars, but stood by to assist when I was in the NDP.

One afternoon we received a visit from a group of six ARVN soldiers. This created some initial confusion. They stepped out of the distant tree line, armed, but carrying their rifles on their shoulders and heading toward our perimeter. The men on guard duty saw them and called down to the company commander. One of them finally contacted our radio operator on a frequency that we had been monitoring and asked for permission to visit our camp. The radio operator checked with battalion and learned that this was an ARVN patrol passing through our area. One of our soldiers advanced to the wire at the edge of the perimeter and escorted them in to meet with the captain and our Vietnamese interpreter.

They were from an ARVN base that was several kilometers away, but still relatively close to us. They were all armed with American-made M-16 rifles. They discussed recent Viet Cong activity and explained that they were on their way to a point farther out in the boonies. The captain gave them a case of C-rations, and they headed back out of our NDP.

Daily life was fairly routine on the days when we did not go out on ambush. We helped unload the supply choppers, cleaned up the area, and performed other miscellaneous duties. On Wednesday, October 9, a couple of Red Cross volunteers visited our camp again. They brought some books, chatted with the guys, and flew off. It was a short visit and there were no medics trying to update shot records.

One of the men in my platoon went into the rear to get his paperwork completed. He was leaving Vietnam in seven days after his one-year tour. He was the first one to go home since I'd been there. It was a great morale booster to see someone make it home safely.

Operating conditions in the camp had stabilized. We now had enough hootches and living space for everyone, and we had finished reinforcing various sections of the camp. The battalion commander wanted more soldiers on patrols, so our mortar platoon began operating like an infantry platoon and went out on daytime missions every third day. We would still leave a squad behind to man at least one mortar if needed. On our first search and destroy patrol, we were joined by a scout dog and his handler. It was always a good start to a patrol when we were joined by a scout dog team, because they provided an additional level of protection. The dogs could sense an ambush or trip wire before we walked into it by alerting their handler with a silent signal such as crossing their ears or stopping and standing on their hind legs.

The army used German shepherds because of their good temperament and ability to adapt to a variety of climates, including the hot, damp climate of Vietnam. The dogs were large and muscular and weighed about seventy-five pounds. The dogs and handlers came from the 35th Infantry platoon (scout dog) based in Di An. The demand for teams of scout dogs and handlers was greater than the supply, so we only received their assistance for about 10 percent of our missions.

The scout dogs were normally near the front of the file while on patrol. When the dog alerted his handler, the word was passed back to the platoon leader who advised everyone to halt temporarily or move forward with greater caution. That day's patrol turned out to be pretty quiet, but over the course of a year I saw numerous instances when the dogs gave us advance warning of trip wires from booby traps and punji pits buried in holes and covered with grass or leaves.

While on patrol, most men carried the standard weapons issued by the army. A couple of men, however, preferred to use nonstandard weapons. One soldier carried a shotgun rather than the standard issue M-16 rifle. No one was quite sure where he obtained the shotgun, because he was not allowed to bring it in from the States. We believed that he purchased it from someone in-country, either in a village or from a GI in another combat unit. In addition to the shotgun, he also carried several boxes of shotgun shells. He believed that the shotgun provided better protection in a close combat situation. It had a wide shot dispersion and provided a better chance of hitting an enemy soldier and stopping him—or at least slowing him down—compared to a rifle that had to be aimed directly at the target. The only significant disadvantage I could see was that it was necessary to open the barrel and insert a new shell each time he fired. This extra time could be critical in a firefight.

Several men in the platoon shared his view and were happy to be close to him on night ambush positions. In most situations where the ambush was blown, we were firing blindly at a general zone in front of us. His shot pattern probably had a greater chance of hitting something.

While I understood his views, I was happy to rely on my M-16. It fired eighteen rounds in rapid succession and sprayed a wide area while firing. I could also pull the magazine out quickly and replace it with a new magazine and continue firing. (The magazine for the M-16 actually held twenty rounds, but we learned that the spring mechanism that pushed the rounds to the top of the magazine did not always work perfectly when it was fully loaded. Most of us only loaded eighteen rounds to ensure that it worked smoothly every time).

One of the lieutenants also had an odd favorite weapon of choice. He carried an old M-1 carbine rifle that he had obtained from an ARVN soldier. He liked the weapon because it was three inches shorter and two pounds lighter than the M-16. The US Army had authorized the M-1 in the early years of the Vietnam War, so ammunition was still available from the normal supply channels. We suspected that he also liked the weapon because it contributed to an aura of individual bravado that he wanted to convey to the men in his platoon.

We had a hectic day on Thursday, October 10. At 12:00 we got word that there were VC on a certain river. Choppers came in and picked up the rest of the company from the area they were patrolling and flew them to this new position. They also wanted the mortar platoon out there to operate as another infantry platoon, so at 12:30 we were airborne and on our way. We spent the rest of the afternoon sweeping the target area but were unable to find any signs of the enemy. Finally, the order came down to set up a pickup zone in a large field and wait for the choppers that were due to pick us up at 17:00. Other missions delayed the choppers, so they were not inbound until

19:00 when they finally headed toward us. It was almost dark by then, and the pilots had difficulty seeing our position. We usually popped violet or green smoke for the choppers, but this time we popped yellow, and they still had difficulty seeing us. They finally landed and flew us back to our NDP. We were thankful, because if another half hour had passed, we would have been forced to spend the night out there. The helicopters didn't land at night unless it was a medevac. It was just about dark by the time we returned to the NDP. The choppers looked impressive at night with red, green, and white running lights on the sides and the tail of each ship.

We found out that the choppers were late because they had picked up another company farther north at Lai-Khe (pronounced LIE-KAY). Just as they were about to take off, the VC mortared them, and a couple of the ships suffered a few holes. As far as we knew, no one was injured.

The evening in camp took a turn for the better. I was feeling pretty good that night, because I played cards after chow and won $16.85. I was a conservative player and allowed fifteen dollars a month for card losses. I liked to think of it as an entertainment expense. At that point I was ahead $2.30 for the month of October. The first month I won eighty-five cents, but last month I lost about sixteen dollars, so I was sort of breaking even.

We heard some bad news from our main base camp, Di An, which was mortared that night. One man was killed, and thirteen more were wounded. As I'd mentioned before, Di An was a very large base, with an airfield and numerous buildings. That place was so large that three-quarters of those people woke up that morning and weren't even aware that the base had been hit.

Our mortar platoon was busy again rebuilding and reinforcing the camp, and everyone was exhausted from digging and filling sandbags. We also went out on patrols and were extremely tired. We had been focused on defending the NDP with mortars, supporting the other line platoons with mortar fire, and going out on night ambushes, but the priorities kept changing.

The following night, we were out on ambush again. It rained for the first two hours, but it cleared up for the rest of the night. The next morning just before dawn, I heard something moving about five feet away. I quietly moved the safety off my rifle and started to raise it when a rat jumped up and ran past me. I'm glad I didn't have my finger on the trigger, or I could have started a hell of a wake-up call. Half an hour later, we picked up our gear and walked back to the NDP.

Speaking of rain, it is one thing that separates the life of a GI from everyone else. When a GI sees rain coming, he just groans and prepares for a miserable time. All he can do is just sit there and get wet. We were freezing all night, but there was nothing we could do but wait for morning to arrive. It was frustrating and disheartening.

There was an interesting diversion at our NDP on one of our stand-downs. It was important that the perimeter be free of any obstructions to ensure a clear field of vision from the edge of the wire all the way out to the tree line in all directions. There was a small tree standing in this no-man's zone. The tree had been ignored when we first arrived, but the foliage had apparently grown thicker and could be used to provide concealment for a Viet Cong who might try to advance on our position. It had been decided that the tree must go.

The platoon sergeant thought this tree removal project was an opportunity to work on his demolition skills. He had someone dig a small hole under the base of the tree then pack a couple of pounds of C-4 explosive in the hole. He inserted a blasting cap in the C-4 then ran the wire back behind one of our bunkers inside the camp. He yelled "fire in the hole" and squeezed the detonator. The resulting blast threw a pile of dirt, smoke, and tree debris fifty feet in the air.

When the dust settled, the tree was now lying on its side, next to a small crater in the ground.

A couple of soldiers carried handsaws out to the fallen tree and cut it into smaller pieces. The trunk was not very thick, so these same handsaws could have cut the tree down in about twenty minutes. There was a curious fascination with explosions and blowing things up, so everyone agreed that the chosen solution was the best one. The visual obstruction had been eliminated, and we were able to blow up a tree.

When we completed the tree removal and cleaned our weapons, we moved to the site of a new bunker that was being built on one edge of our camp. The engineers gave us several lengths of six-by-six-inch timbers that provided the main support for the structure. A chain saw somehow magically appeared and was used to trim the timbers to the correct lengths, and they were connected to form the frame of the bunker. Once again, a large sandbag detail was assembled to produce the sandbags that formed the walls and roof of this structure. By the end of the day, the new structure was 50 percent complete. We'd be going out on more patrols in the next few days, so the completion would have to wait until our next stand-down. The platoon sergeant and the lieutenant were pleased with the progress.

Most of us were happy to receive any mail and especially happy to receive a package. I continued to receive packages from home about once a week, some from my mother, some from my fiancée, and others from various relatives. The latest package included a pocketknife, nail clipper, packets of dry lemonade mix, a box of cookies, and several cans of deviled ham. I headed over to the mess tent and grabbed a couple of slices of bread to make a deviled ham sandwich—a tasty change from the normal menu. One of our buddies received a package from his girlfriend and started to grumble and complain. We asked why he was upset. He pointed to the package in his hands, and we saw the product name in bold letters: "Travel Alarm Clock." He grumbled and said, "I don't need a damn alarm clock. I need some sleep." We joked about it and decided that if this was the worst thing that happened that day, we all considered ourselves pretty lucky. He reluctantly agreed.

There was an accident on Tuesday, October 15. One of the men was burning trash at the far end of the camp. While he was pouring gasoline on the trash pile he spilled some on his feet. Several men raced to help him and managed to smother the flames quickly, but his legs were pretty badly burned. The medevac chopper flew him to a hospital that handled burn cases. This incident was not directly combat related, so he wouldn't get a purple heart. We also heard that he wouldn't be returning. When his legs healed, he would get a discharge. There were a number of similar accidental incidents throughout the year, probably a consequence of a large group of young guys taking risks in a venture already full of life-threatening risks.

Tuesday turned out to be a very unlucky day. We were tired much of the time, with patrols during the day or ambushes at night. When I was lucky enough to be in the base camp, I slept pretty soundly in my hootch. Even the firing of our mortars didn't wake me, because they went off frequently at night in support of other units out on ambush or firing H&I missions. H&I was "harassing and interdicting," the firing of mortar or artillery rounds at random positions that have been identified as enemy targets. The targets were road or river junctions where enemy movement had recently been spotted. Since there was a curfew, no one was supposed to be moving at night, and we knew where our own forces were positioned.

I awoke in the middle of one of these fire missions, because the normal thump sound of the round leaving the tube was followed by a nearby blast and then the shouts of several men. I jumped out of my cot, grabbed my rifle and helmet, and ran out. My first thought was that Viet Cong were attacking our position. I soon learned that we were not being attacked, but that we had experienced a "short" round inside our perimeter near the cook's hootch. Several cooks and a couple of other men were wounded from the blast of the HE (high explosive) round. The medics quickly assessed the wounded and determined that a few of them needed to be medevaced to a hospital for treatment. A short time later the medevac helicopter arrived at the landing zone in our perimeter and took off with the wounded. Fortunately, no one was killed.    They all survived their wounds and returned to duty in the coming days and weeks.

A word about a "short" round: The mortar round has a series of cloth pouches attached to the base near the fin. There are as many as nine pouches that are attached. If fewer pouches are needed because of a shorter distance to the target, they will be pulled off the round by the gunner before dropping the round into the tube.

Occasionally, the pouches became damp and did not burn. This reduced the force of the blast in the tube and resulted in the round falling short of its target. We took precautions to keep these rounds dry, but we were fighting a war in a country with a monsoon season. We also understood that war is an imperfect enterprise, and this was one of the risks of living and working in a war zone.

The next morning we saw two more casualties from this accident. Two of the water tubs used to wash dishes were riddled with shrapnel holes and out of commission. These were large metal garbage cans with burners placed underneath. Three of them were filled with water and then heated. When soldiers had finished their meals they were required to dip their metal trays in three successive tubs. The first had soapy water, the second had rinse water, and the last one had water with some type of sanitizer added. The two "wounded" cans were scrapped and replaced with new ones on the next supply chopper.

# CHAPTER 8

# VIET CONG BUNKER COMPLEX

My fiancée sent me a puzzle consisting of four plastic blocks that were twisted, so the various colors wound up in a specific sequence, a precursor to the Rubik's cube. I worked on the puzzle for four days before getting it to come out right. One of the guys had been very lucky at cards lately and had been blowing his own horn quite a bit to the annoyance of many. I thought I would try to bring this guy down a peg and gave him the blocks. I told him that I'd give him fifteen dollars if he could solve the puzzle within forty-eight hours. I figured he'd go crazy and stay up all night trying to solve it. Well, he completed the puzzle in five minutes, and the whole platoon broke out laughing. This undertaking backfired, so I decided to stop making bets for a while.

We spent most of that day fixing up our hootches by adding more sheets of plastic and piling dirt around the walls to waterproof them as much as possible. It had rained most of the day, and a typhoon was headed our way within the next twenty-four hours. There was a definite sense of urgency.

By Sunday, October 20, the typhoon had come and gone. It had been blowing and raining very hard all night. Several hootches were blown apart, because the wind ripped open the poncho/plastic roof sheets on the structures, and the men were soaked. Thanks to our careful preparation, our hootch stayed safe and dry. Some of our good luck was due to the fact that it was smaller and shorter. The storm finally stopped around noon, and the skies cleared up. In spite of the damage to some of the hootches, no one was injured.

At 21:30 we heard firing in the distance. A South Vietnamese army training base about two miles from us was hit by mortars. We heard them call for assistance on the battalion radio. A couple of helicopter gunships were on the way, so the VC would stop firing soon to avoid being blown away.

We had an interesting day on Tuesday, October 22. I was in the camp during the day when the Apollo 7 astronauts returned to earth and landed safely. This was the mission with Walter Schirra, Donn Eisele, and Walter Cunningham. We heard it live on AFVN radio.

That day was also the changeover day for money. Every GI in Vietnam turned in all his MPC (military payment certificates) and received a receipt. In two or three days, we were reimbursed with a new issue of certificates for an equivalent amount. The only people allowed to turn in the money were GIs and American personnel. The purpose of the currency changeover was to slow down black market activities. All the South Vietnamese people who had the old MPC were now stuck with worthless paper. This included a lot of short-time girls, although I strongly suspected that they were able to get a lot of their money changed by having GIs do it for them in return for a commission. Since we were located out in the boonies, no civilians asked us for assistance with money transfers.

I lost another camera, though not in a river. I was on a garbage detail where we dug a hole to bury garbage in a field near the NDP. I hung the camera on a small tree after taking a picture of an ox outside the wire. We finished digging at 11:00 and headed back to our hootches. I forgot about the camera until about 22:00 that night. I asked if anyone had picked it up, but no one had seen it. It was my own fault but still very frustrating.

The next day I returned to the tree where I had left my camera, but it wasn't there. Half an hour later the company commander called all the platoon leaders together and told them to have a shakedown. I had not requested this, but the officers suspected that someone in our camp had stolen the camera. Everyone was ordered to stand by his hootch with all his gear open. The shakedown had just started when one of the men asked what they were looking for. When he heard that it was a camera, he said that he had found one the night before and brought it over to the ARVN compound a thousand meters from ours. He had gone over there at 20:00 to monitor their radio as scheduled. I then went over to the ARVN compound, and they acknowledged that someone had dropped off a camera that had been found in a field. It was none the worse for wear, and I was glad to have it back.

The good fortune continued into the evening when I received a package in the mail. It was the camera that I had sent to Japan to be repaired. It had been repaired and shipped back, free of charge, even though the guarantee didn't cover accidents. It made my day. I planned to store one of the cameras in my locker back at Di An.

We spent a long night on ambush. We had crossed through the wire in the late afternoon and headed out to our ambush site a couple of klicks from our base camp. We lined up along a raised berm at the edge of a field. A short line of troops assembled along our left flank to protect us from being encircled by the enemy—the classic L-shaped ambush position that we used repeatedly throughout the year. Another platoon set up an ambush position about three hundred meters to our right. We settled in for the night and took turns staying awake watching for movement.

Early in the morning, around 02:00, the other platoon saw movement and blew their ambush. All hell broke loose as they started firing M-16s, M-60s, and M-79 grenade launchers. It was ten minutes of total noise and confusion. Their platoon leader called over to warn us that VC were moving in our direction. Someone in our position saw some movement in front of us and started firing. Instantly, everyone joined in as we sprayed the area in front of us with a blanket of bullets and grenades. The other unit still saw movement between our positions and notified us that they were calling in artillery from a base that was supporting us with 105 mm or 155 mm artillery pieces. We were still firing at the kill zone in front of us, but more selectively as we tried to identify human figures.

Five minutes later, we heard the whining sound of an artillery shell in flight. We all lay flat and dug into the earth. The first shell hit the ground several hundred meters in front of us. It exploded with a bright white flash, and its white phosphorous content provided feedback on its location relative to the target. The FO in the other position sent corrections to the artillery FDC. The next white phosphorous shell landed much closer to our position, about two hundred meters in front of us. We felt a mild vibration in the ground as the force of the shell moved through the earth. The placement of this round satisfied the FO as he sent the command to "fire for effect." The artillery gun crew switched ammunition and now loaded HE (high-explosive) shells into the guns. These shells were designed to explode on impact and unleash a massive wall of metal shrapnel pieces in all directions spreading out from the point of impact. A five-minute barrage of continuous explosions began as the artillery shells tore up the field in front of us and to our right. We now felt heavy movement in the ground as the concussion from each round sent its explosive force rippling through the earth.

It was a terrifying experience for us. The concussions lifted the ground under us, and the deafening noise of each explosion assaulted our ears. I knew that the shells were not meant to harm us, but the shock waves and the noise were overwhelming. I was terrified with a fear and a sense of helplessness that was the worst I was to experience during my entire tour. I felt pity for anyone caught out in that field and could not understand how anyone could survive such a massive assault of firepower.

I was also afraid of being a victim of "friendly fire." There was a line of small palm trees near us on our right flank, and artillery shells were indiscriminate. The fuses had been set to explode on impact, but the shell could not differentiate between the impact of the ground two hundred meters in front of us and the impact of hitting the sturdy trunk of a palm tree right next to us. The shell had no emotion, it simply followed the laws of physics as it left the barrel from the artillery position far behind us. It traveled in a long upward-climbing arc and then curved downward toward its carefully calculated destination, a point in the earth in a field in front of us.

We wanted to have faith that the artillery crew was being precise and correct. We wanted to believe that the FO had called in the correct target position. We wanted to believe that the soldier in the FDC heard the target coordinates correctly. We wanted to believe that the gun crew had sighted the gun correctly and had set the proper elevation. We wanted to trust that they used the correct powder charge to propel the shell the correct distance. We wanted to trust that the powder charge was dry and would explode correctly with the right amount of force. On this night, everyone did his job as he was supposed to. There were no errant rounds, and we had no "friendly fire" casualties.

When the barrage ended, we were ordered to move forward and look for enemy soldiers or casualties. We moved forward cautiously and searched for any signs of movement. We did not like moving through a field at night, where an enemy could start firing at us from anywhere, but this felt like a safer task than hearing and feeling the artillery barrage we had just experienced. So we worked our way across the field. We did not find any Viet Cong or even evidence of their presence. The other platoon also checked the area in front of their position and failed to find any Viet Cong. Was someone really out there? We were no longer certain. The elusiveness of a guerrilla war left us with the possibility that they had escaped the massive firepower from our side or perhaps were never there in the first place. All I knew for certain was that this was my first experience with artillery support at night. It was terrifying, and I will remember this night for the rest of my life. I would relive this experience again on other ambushes, but none would have the personal impact of the first.

It was my turn to go to Di An on Saturday, October 26. Before I left that morning I spent an hour taking group shots of the company commander, the artillery officer, and all the platoon leaders, as well as a group shot of my platoon. I used seven different cameras (belonging to them), and I took a few shots with my camera. I stored the recently repaired camera in my locker at Di An and headed over to the PX. There was a heavily discounted TLR (twin lens reflex) camera on sale. It was better for close-ups, because it provided finer detail. It also had an adapter to shoot either 35 mm film or 120 film, which produced a larger negative to make enlargements with greater clarity.

Living in the middle of an open field meant that we sometimes got very close to nature, including a few rats in our compound. We slept on air mattresses on top of a row of four or five ammo boxes, so we were about ten inches off the ground. The rats usually stayed on the ground and left us alone. However, one rat, "Harvey," had run across my hootchmate's chest twice in the past three weeks. I suggested he should take a shower more often. Nobody had been bitten by a rat, and we did have poison spread around.

The next day, some type of proficiency inspection had been scheduled. A team came out to see how well our platoon handled the mortars. As the FO, I was not directly involved, since we were not actually going to fire the mortars, but I did help with a general cleanup of the area. The mortar platoon inspection went very well. The inspection team confirmed that our men were very efficient and well organized on the guns. A lot of credit went to Sergeant Moore, who made a point of maintaining technical proficiency in all aspects of this platoon.

We learned that half our platoon would continue to go out on daytime patrols with the regular line platoons each day. The company was required to have ninety men in the field every day, and we had lost several due to injuries recently. We alternated the daytime patrols; half to go out in the field and the other half to stay back and man the mortars if needed.

I received a letter from Christina on October 27. She was driving with a friend when they had an accident. The friend slammed on the brakes on a rain-slick highway to avoid hitting another car, and they swerved out of control. Both were cut up and bruised, but they walked away from the car, which was a total wreck. X-rays disclosed no broken bones, so she was in good shape and pretty lucky. In an interesting coincidence, the doctor who treated her at the hospital had spent some time in the "Big Red One" in World War II. It's a small world.

Sergeant Moore, anxious for a new project, determined that we needed a solid floor under the FDC tent that would not get muddy when it rained. He filled out the appropriate requisitions and received a couple of trowels, some long-handled shovels, and several bags of cement mix from one of the resupply deliveries carried in by the Chinook.

He formed a work detail that proceeded to build forms for a concrete pad using the wood from ammo boxes. They also built a four-foot-by-four-foot wooden box in which cement, sand, and water were mixed together until it reached a thick consistency. Individual wooden ammo boxes were used to transport the mix and pour it into the pad frame. We completed the job in about four hours.

With the leftover cement the crew took this opportunity to create the letter "M," for "Mortar," our specialty in the camp, using wooden frames. We decorated it with five-inch plastic caps from the cardboard tubes that held our mortar shells by placing them in the wet concrete.

As the concrete M started to dry and harden, someone suggested a brighter color than the plain gray. One of the craftsmen pulled the pin on a violet color smoke grenade, attached a six inch wire to the canister and moved it slowly over the concrete M. He continued "painting" the M until the smoke grenade had exhausted all of its purple smoke. It was the perfect finishing touch. Everyone in the platoon stopped to check out our new logo. We felt that we had left a permanent mark at this camp.

I received my orders confirming that I would be receiving a CIB, the Combat Infantryman Badge awarded to infantry soldiers after spending ninety days in a combat zone. It was a silver rifle on a blue badge with a wreath around it.

On November 1, President Johnson's speech about the bombing halt was broadcast live at 09:30 local time on AFVN radio. All work in the camp ceased as we listened intently. I was not too surprised about the bombing halt, but I was surprised that the NLF (National Liberation Front—the political arm of the Viet Cong in South Vietnam) was invited to sit in on the Paris talks, even though they were not formally recognized. Apparently the United States was willing to make some concessions. While trying to be objective,

I couldn't help but resent the coincidence that the next Paris talks were being held at the same time as the US elections. My level of cynicism increased when I saw the people in power playing games with entire nations and millions of people. The bombing halt of North Vietnam had no immediate effect on our mission, so we continued to go out on search and destroy patrols during the day and ambush patrols during the night.

The next day we boarded the choppers for another search and destroy mission. We were joined by a Kit Carson scout who had been assigned to our unit. These scouts were former Viet Cong soldiers who had agreed to assist the American army. There had been reports of recent VC activity in an area that had been the scene of several engagements in the past year. As we headed into the landing zone, we saw the familiar circular pools of water that were the craters left by artillery shells blasting holes into the ground. It was a quiet LZ (landing zone) with no resistance, but everyone was alert and moving carefully as we landed, quickly left the field, and headed out along our designated route.

It was typical of most of our recent patrols, with lots of wet, muddy fields, thick clumps of palm trees, and bushes along small rivers and tributaries. We crossed a couple of narrow rivers without incident, but there was an air of expectancy as we continued to move through vegetation that seemed thicker and denser than normal.

Suddenly, the Kit Carson scout stopped and pointed to something up ahead. He was near the front of the file, and everyone dropped to the ground and did a 360 degree check of our surroundings. We continued to advance slowly for about fifty feet then stopped again. A small group advanced another fifty feet then passed the word that we were near a VC camp. More troops moved forward, and two other groups moved to the left and right of the camp location. The advance group determined that no enemy soldiers were in the camp, so we continued to advance until the camp was surrounded. It was obvious that this was an enemy camp, because we were deep in the boonies with no roads or villages anywhere near this location. Several soldiers continued to slowly advance to the center of the encampment while carefully checking for trip wires and booby traps. None were found.

There was no fire burning in the camp, but someone found a small pot of rice that was still warm. It appeared that the camp had been occupied until just a short time before we arrived. Perhaps one of the VC lookouts heard our helicopters land a couple of hours earlier or observed our patrol moving toward them. We believed they abandoned the camp in a great hurry because of the items that they left behind.

We found a small structure about five feet tall, made of bamboo poles and covered with palm fronds, that provided some protection from rain, sun, and observation by our helicopters that might fly overhead. It had a floor made with several wooden planks. Inside, our Vietnamese scout found several large tins of rice and other food and a plastic bag filled with some type of beans. He broke into a bright smile as he opened the bag and started to eat them. There were also several buckets of fresh water and a variety of pots, pans, and utensils. Someone uncovered an old rifle and some ammunition; someone else found a 60 mm mortar manufactured by one of the communist bloc countries. There was no ammunition for the mortar. Everything we found was typical of what we expected to see in a VC camp.

Then we began to find some unusual items. There was a quart jar filled with liquid mercury that could be used to make switches to set off charges or explosive devices when moved. There was a portable typewriter in perfect condition inside a carrying case. We also found several notebooks in binders and a variety of other documents that were packed in plastic bags. The most unusual items were long rolls of what appeared to be movie film strewn among some trees, possibly in an attempt to destroy the film before they left. We found a newspaper, *Giai Phong*, which meant freedom or liberation. We relayed the location of the camp and a summary of the contents to battalion. They were happy to learn of the find and were eager to examine the items we had found. We finally gathered up all of the captured items and resumed our patrol. We later learned that the camp we uncovered was the base for some type of propaganda unit of the Viet Cong.

Later in the afternoon we found a second bunker complex, a VC sampan, a rifle, and three mortar rounds. Then, just as we were getting ready to move to our pickup zone, we found a third bunker complex and a 60 mm mortar. Battalion decided to leave us there to pull an all-night ambush. We were not thrilled with this order, but we had no choice in the matter. We had, after all, found more direct evidence of local Viet Cong activity in one day than we had seen in the last three weeks. They flew in fresh water and C-rations, and we set up for the night.

It was just after sundown as one of our men was setting out his claymore in front of his position when somebody started talking to him in Vietnamese. As it turned out there was a squad of VC moving through the area. The VC that was talking to our man thought that he was another VC, and he kept repeating a phrase as if he was asking for a countersign. Our soldier stood there for a minute and then started slowly walking back to our position. He had just reached our line when the VC clicked his weapon off safe. Then all hell broke loose. The VC started firing at us, and all of our rifles, machine guns, and grenade launchers were firing back. Everyone detonated their claymores, and then artillery was called in. The firing went on intermittently for an hour, although the VC took off as soon as they realized that they had walked into an ambush. The rest of the night remained quiet, although no one got a lot of sleep since we were still on high alert. We swept the area the next morning but found nothing. The VC had taken their dead and wounded with them. None of our people were wounded, in spite of the fact that we saw that the trees behind us were riddled with holes. The choppers came in, and we were flown out of there at 08:00.

A Vietnamese Kit Carson scout points to the name of the newspaper, *Liberation*, captured, along with other supplies, in a Viet Cong bunker complex.

Rice and weapons are discovered.

The Kit Carson scout checks for trip wires and booby traps in the bunker complex.

# CHAPTER 9

# BRONZE STARS AND COMMENDATION MEDALS

One afternoon a new man asked about the availability of liquor. We were not allowed to have hard liquor, but there was beer at the main camp in Di An. We weren't supposed to have beer at the NDP either, but every couple of days, somebody managed to smuggle a case or two on the supply chopper. Sometimes they put it in a duffel bag or a rucksack. Other times they put beer cans in a soda case and sent it with the rest of the sodas. The mess tent received some ice each day to preserve the food and used some of the ice to keep a modest number of sodas (or beer) cool. Since there was very little beer available for all of the men in this camp, we rarely had a problem with someone being drunk or unfit for duty. If we were caught with hard liquor, there were two possibilities: either split the bottle with whoever caught you, or receive an article 15 (nonjudicial punishment), which would probably be forfeiture of a month's pay.

In early November we conducted a check of the perimeter defense. Our base in the clearing was surrounded by a ring of concertina wire that was rolled out in coils with razor-sharp barbs designed to slow someone down if they tried to cross through or over the wire. We also had claymore mines set in place facing outside the wire. The M-18A1 claymore mine was made of a curved solid plastic frame about eleven inches wide and five inches tall. It contained about seven hundred steel balls and was packed with C-4 explosive. When the mine was detonated it sent out a spray of steel balls to a distance of about one hundred meters. The mine held a blasting cap that was connected to a wire that ran back to our bunkers and was fired by squeezing a plastic "clacker" that sent an electric charge to the blasting cap.

One of the most important defensive elements was a series of foo gas containers that were buried just outside the wire perimeter. This was part of the final protective fire line that was to be used when the camp was under attack and in danger of being overrun. Foo gas was a mixture of explosives and napalm stored in fifty-gallon drums. It was ignited by a remote-control wire that went back to the bunkers. When detonated it released a large cloud of flaming napalm that covered an area of several hundred meters.

Sergeant Moore called out a warning that he was about to test fire one of the foo gas barrels. Everyone in the camp got behind protective cover as he yelled, "Fire in the hole!" and ignited the barrel. The sound of the blast was followed by a bright yellow-orange cloud of flame that rose over a large area of the perimeter and then fell to the ground, igniting small grass fires in several spots. This was followed by a large black cloud of smoke that rose slowly above the blast site. The flames continued to burn for another ten or fifteen minutes in various spots in the field. We understood that this was a last line of defense if we were attacked by a ground force, the final barrier that an enemy would have to overcome. It would be devastating for any individual caught in that blanket of flame. We ventured out to check the effect of this weapon. If the opposing force was large enough, the remaining troops would rush through the field after the blast and be on us. Our only defense in that event would be our small arms weapons. We hoped we would not have to face that extreme situation. The following day a new barrel of foo gas was brought in to replace the one that had been tested.

We went out on another search and destroy mission that was much longer than usual. We crossed two rivers and hacked our way with machetes through some very thick growth. We covered quite a bit of ground, and it was nearly dark when we made it back to camp. It was the night of the 1968 US elections, and there was a chance that we would be hit, so we slept with our flak jackets and helmets.

It turned out to be a pretty close election and was followed with careful attention among the troops, especially since the returns were broadcast live. It was nighttime in New York, but it was daytime in Vietnam. We had a large sheet of plastic nailed to a stack of ammo boxes that showed the updated returns on an hourly basis. There were columns of state names followed by the candidate who won each state. Individuals took turns updating the results using a black grease pencil to show the popular vote and the electoral vote for the three candidates: Nixon, Humphrey, and Wallace. It was Wednesday, November 6, and Nixon became our new president. At the time, I was encouraged and felt that he would be the best person to manage this war.

Life in the camp could be pretty mellow in the early evening when we were not on some type of alert. If we didn't go out on a night ambush, we used the time to read, listen to the radio, or write letters. There was no electricity in this camp, so the hootches were illuminated with candles or individual flashlights. As I wandered around, I often noticed a pungent sweet smell coming from the cook's hootch. Some guys occasionally stopped by to hang around for a few drags of marijuana before heading back to their own space.

Most members of the company did not openly use drugs, but the cooks seemed to have a different attitude. They did not usually carry rifles, and their jobs were not critical to their survival. If they got high, the oatmeal might be thick and lumpy in the morning, or the scrambled eggs might be runny, but they weren't firing a weapon over the head of a buddy crawling through a rice paddy. Admittedly, there were some infantry and mortar soldiers who seemed to be in a daze on some nights when we were in the base camp.

In our unit, most of us avoided drugs, because we were near the midpoint of the war and still wanted to believe that we were making a difference in the future of South Vietnam and the United States. The most important reason was the prospect that we might have to engage the enemy on very short notice. I was determined to stay alive and avoid the risk of being less than alert at any time.

In the years after I left Vietnam, reports of heavy drug use seemed to increase in direct proportion to the belief that the war was a lost cause, because the number of troops serving in-country dropped dramatically. It was also a reflection of antiwar protests and increased drug use back home. The respect for officers and noncoms also declined rapidly in the early seventies, with growing incidents of fragging[3] and the outright killing of officers who were too enthusiastic about risky missions. But in the year that I served, and in my company, drug use was light, and everyone tried to do his best to get through his tour with the least amount of hassle and risk. We just wanted to get home in one piece and get on with our lives.

Our mission was canceled at the last minute on November 7, but we would be going out the following day. My mood changed from day to day, and that day was one of the bad days. I was getting a little stir-crazy and just wanted to get the hell out of there. I don't think that it was Vietnam that was bothering me as much as that base camp. The only real contact that we had with civilization was the supply chopper that came in twice a day. It was harder to get into Di An because of the weight restrictions of the supply chopper. We usually sent one man back to Di An each day on a rotating basis,

---

3  Fragging, the practice of pulling the pin on a fragmentation grenade and throwing it into an officer's hootch.

but it had been a long time since I had been able to go. If it wasn't for mail and the radio, I think that I might have cracked up. Another issue was the lack of contact with anyone other than fellow soldiers at the camp. There were a couple of kids who went by with their water buffalo every day, but that was about it.

We finally headed out on another uneventful search and destroy mission. It turned out to be pretty tedious, but I was not looking for too much excitement involving enemy fire. When we returned, I received a package with fifteen hundred black-and-white pictures I had ordered from the base photo shop. I started sorting them and then passed them on to the men in the platoon, including my platoon sergeant, who was now a customer.

On Saturday, November 9, we were told to clean up and look sharp. A colonel flew in from battalion, and we assembled in formation. He made a short speech acknowledging our continued success in meeting the goals of our mission and proceeded to award medals to the men in our company. He awarded six Bronze Star medals and four Army Commendation medals. In addition, there were several Purple Hearts and nearly fifteen Combat Infantryman Badges (CIB) given out. Most of the Bronze Star and Army Commendation medals were for action that had taken place just prior to my joining this company.

Before the ceremony, the company commander informed me that I would be receiving my CIB medal later, because he thought that I would be taking pictures during the ceremony. This was a good turn of events for all concerned. I could take some great shots of men being recognized for their service, and he thought it would be good for morale if they could have a photo to send home that showed them receiving a medal.

It continued to surprise me that everyone thought I knew so much about cameras. In one week four different men brought me their cameras to fix, but reluctantly I had to tell them that I had neither the equipment nor the know-how to fix a camera and advised them to send their cameras to the manufacturer for repairs.

The following day we had a smaller ceremony in our platoon. We did not have a colonel presiding, but it was just as important for the men involved. The soldier who had been working as the lead man in the FDC was rotating home that day. He had been working with his replacement for the past three weeks and was ready to leave.

It was a tradition started a few years earlier that the current reigning FDC identified his position with a "rod of honor." The rod was a varnished staff about three feet long with a brass tip at the bottom and a dragonhead at the top. The rod was not entirely unique to our platoon, since many of the shops in the villages sold them for a modest price. The rod in our platoon, however, had been endowed with special significance and was treated with reverence. The primary job of the FDC was to identify the location of a mortar target on a map and calculate the direction, elevation, and size of charge for hitting the target. The job was important, because a mistake in the calculations could result in a mortar round landing in front or in back of the target, possibly hitting friendly troops that had requested the fire support.

At the appointed hour, the outbound FDC grabbed his pack and gear and stood in front of one of the mortar pits. A second soldier knelt on the ground and held up a small board that was covered with a clean towel. The rod of honor was resting on the towel. The incoming FDC approached the rod and the towel and faced the other FDC. A small group from the mortar platoon gathered around to witness the transition. The outbound FDC stated that it had been his honor to serve with this platoon and the men in it, and he expressed his wish that we would all get through our tours as safely as he had. He then expressed confidence in the new FDC, picked up the rod of honor and passed it to his replacement. The new man expressed his gratitude at being appointed to the position and promised to do his best to keep everyone safe. There was a general round of applause, and the ceremony was over.

A foo gas container was tested at the NDP. Barrels containing a mixture of explosives and napalm were placed in a ring around the camp as a final defensive barrier in the event of an attack.

Medals are awarded during a ceremony at the NDP.

A member of the company receives a Bronze Star and the Army Commendation Medal.

A few minutes later the resupply Chinook flew in, and the departing FDC boarded the chopper to go back to the main base at Di An. Eventually he'd be going back to the States. We were always happy to see a man go home, because it reaffirmed our belief and hope that we would also make it home at some point in the future.

About this time the rumor mill reported that we would be heading north to the Cambodian border in January. Time would tell how accurate this prediction was. There was much concern about another Tet offensive in mid-February, and we were already making preparations.

They flew in cement and sand on the Chinook, and we spent the day building a cement floor for the mess area. We used water from an old well, so we didn't have to use any of our drinking water.

One of the men in our platoon received a letter from his wife and he shared the part that was of personal interest. "...by the way, tell the guy who's been taking those big black-and-white photos that he's a good photographer. He is! His pictures of you are good, and the background is good, too. All that elephant grass and even a palm tree. He showed how thick the jungle is in a few of the pictures. That one of the three of you talking while you were eating rations was very good. Tell him I said thanks an awful lot for bringing you closer to me through his pictures and helping me see what it looks like and how life is for you guys over there. Really now, thank him for me."

A letter like that made it worth the two cameras in the river. In fact, it made the whole thing worthwhile. I gave him a little note to send her in his next letter thanking her for her thoughts. That letter really broke me up, and I felt more "involved" than I had been for a long time.

The next day we received some bad news. It was my turn to stay back in the camp, but half of our platoon and the rest of the company went out on a search and destroy mission. One of the men from another platoon was dismantling a booby trap when the blasting cap went off in his hand. It blew his hand apart, and he was dusted off. They had no other enemy contact for the rest of the day.

I was part of the group that went out on patrol the following day, and we found several VC bunkers with concrete floors. This indicated a degree of permanence not usually found this far south. We also found a couple of RPGs (rocket-propelled grenades) and twenty-four pounds of plastic explosive. There were two booby traps at the site that were dismantled safely. Later on, as we were heading for our pickup zone, we were temporarily stopped. As I checked our rear to see if anyone was following us, out of the corner of my eye I saw the other guys dropping to the ground. I hit the ground so fast that my helmet rolled off. The point man had just missed stepping on another booby trap. It was a Chinese grenade tied to a stake, with a string running from the pin across the trail to a tree. These damn booby traps were popping up more and more often. We continued to the pickup zone without further incident.

When we returned to the NDP, we cleaned up and ate. The mood was more serious, given the events of the last two days. Five or six of us were talking casually about the usual topics, and then I started asking more serious questions about life in general and our expectations after we leave Vietnam. Things like "Are you happy?"; "What does success in life mean to you?" It turned into one of the deepest conversations since I'd arrived there. We talked until 01:00 the next morning. The honesty with which each man expressed himself was very surprising to me. I am not suggesting that combat situations are necessary for individuals to review what is truly important in their lives, but on that evening, everyone shared very personal thoughts and beliefs. It felt like we were participating in an encounter group without any moderators. The group decided which comments were the most meaningful and then followed that topic until another subject led in a different direction. We developed a deeper understanding of one another than we had before.

Wednesday, November 13, brought some good news. I received my orders confirming a change in rank from spec-4 to sergeant (E-5). My MOS also changed from 11B20 to 11B40. There was no immediate change in my duties, although I anticipated I would be asked to be a squad leader in a few weeks. I would also be getting a small bump in pay, but I was still an infantryman.

A couple of pets began to appear in our base camp. One of the soldiers was feeding a small, light-brown puppy. Another man had a small monkey on a thin leash that he kept near his hootch. Both animals were purchased from local Vietnamese eager to get some cash. The monkey turned out to be a real star. Everyone enjoyed playing with him and having his picture taken with him.

Official army policy did not permit animals or pets on base, but we were in the boondocks actively patrolling and engaging the enemy, so we were allowed some slack. We did not polish our boots, stand for inspection in the morning, or participate in PT drills. On warm days we were able to walk around in a pair of green boxer shorts and sandals in the base camp. It was an unwritten rule that there was a fair amount of personal freedom in off-duty hours if you were in the field, especially if you were infantry. Back in the "rear" at Di An, everyone wore a full set of fatigues. Their boots tended to see a shoeshine brush more often, but even there, the degree of military formality tended to vary exponentially with the physical distance from battalion headquarters.

We tried to look reasonably neat even in the field, so we shaved and showered when we had the opportunity. Haircuts were more difficult to obtain. Occasionally we would get a day to go back to Di An on the Chinook supply chopper. There was a barbershop on the base, staffed by Vietnamese women who did a good job of barbering at a low price. We could visit the company barber in our base camp. Though not an official barber, he had some training in civilian life and had his barber tools. When he had free time, he'd cut your hair for fifty cents or barter for some snack food from home. He did a good job, and the neat look of most troops kept visiting brass from hassling the officers and noncoms with needless grief.

While a GI was getting his hair trimmed, someone else would often use his spare time to practice on a guitar. The music was welcome and made the place seem more like a refuge from the grimmer realities outside the wire. The amount of gear that you could bring over here was limited. Guitars were large items, but in spite of this, three or four guitars in the company were heard at different times of the day. There were several radios in the platoon, one belonged to my hootchmate. We listened to broadcasts on AFVN radio which played a mix of popular hits.

We set out on another patrol, and it turned out to be a pretty good day. We completed the entire route we were scheduled to patrol and reached our pickup point early, around 14:00. Near the pickup point we came across a crater that was thirty feet in diameter and about twelve feet deep. It had been made by a five-hundred-pound bomb and had filled with water. Since we had to wait for the choppers anyway, we stopped at this spot. Several men volunteered to set up security. The rest of us took off our gear and our shirts. We spent the next hour and a half swimming, and we had a ball. You could dive straight down from the edge with no worry about hitting the bottom. Maybe war isn't *all* hell.

On Friday, November 15, we had an unexpected surprise. We got an opportunity to watch *Rowan & Martin's Laugh-In* and the *Combat* show. One of the sergeants had purchased a portable television and brought it out to the NDP. He ran it on the same batteries that we used in the field radios. The programs were broadcast on AFVN (Armed Forces Vietnam Network) and came out of Saigon on channel 11. The *Laugh-In* show was very funny, and we enjoyed seeing American women, even if only on TV. I also liked Judy Carne because of her cute British accent. We especially enjoyed *Combat*, the World War II series, because we could point out all the mistakes that the characters made on patrols, like bunching up together, making them an inviting target.

Our next search and destroy mission was uneventful. The foliage was getting pretty dry as the rainy season ended, so we started fires to burn the grasses and brush in the fields that were farther away from villages or out in the boonies. This was to deprive the enemy of places to hide. The elephant grass usually burned pretty quickly, but the palm trees and bushes didn't burn unless they were dead.

One of our men found a couple of VC propaganda leaflets directed at US servicemen. This was the first time I had seen these since I arrived. One leaflet read, "GI! If anyone invaded your country, massacred your compatriots, destroyed your homes, villages, and property, how would you react against all that? The South Vietnamese people love peace, but they love freedom and independence still more! It is why they are rising to take arms to oppose US aggressors and the traitors to the nation! Don't make the South Vietnamese people hate you! They are not enemies of your people! Your lives are precious. Your family, your wife, and your children need you. You must not let Washington decide by itself your own destiny in serving the selfish ambition of the US warmongers and their stooges!"

Another said, "GI! The contention that 'The Americans oppose the Vietnamese who aggress Vietnam on the Vietnamese Territory' is nothing but a farce! Is it conceivable that you, an educated and fair-minded person, believe the deceitful contentions of Johnson, McNamara? Why sacrifice your youthful days to bury your honor and life in the South Vietnamese battlefields? Oppose the US aggressive war in South Vietnam! Repatriate the US Expeditionary Corps! Peace for Vietnam!"

The leaflets looked pretty new, but were not current, because McNamara had already resigned as secretary of defense in February of that year. We dismissed the leaflets as enemy propaganda.

Since she was receiving most of my photos, Christina asked me if we were allowed to take photos of enemy supplies, etc. We were allowed to photograph enemy supplies, weapons etc. I was cautioned, however, about taking photos of our own supply depots or ammunition stockpiles. I also told her that we had some time to read books, since there were not a lot of other entertainment options available. I had read *Brave New World* in high school, but a couple of the men were discussing the book, so I decided to read it again. At that time I was also reading *Capable of Honor* by Allen Drury.

I had a great day on Wednesday, November 20. We conducted a "medcap." We went into a nearby village with a couple of medics or doctors, plenty of medical supplies, and lots of candy for the kids. We had a great time, and I took loads of pictures. The villagers made large pottery jars in addition to harvesting rice, fishing, and raising cows and pigs.

In the afternoon, one family invited me into their home to share a feast they had prepared. I couldn't believe my eyes. The table was covered with over twenty tasty and appetizing dishes. I tried several, and they were delicious. The menu included all sorts of roots, beans, and crayfish, etc. The men were dining at the table, and the women kept busy replenishing the food. They served bottled Vietnamese beer and some local brew of homemade whiskey. I had a glass of the beer, but I didn't trust the whiskey.

We had been instructed not to eat any of the local foods for fear of hepatitis or other ailments, but this food looked so good, and it was freshly cooked. I'm sorry now that I didn't try everything. One of the mama-sans served a little cake. It looked like a very fine white angel food cake with pink-swirl sweetening on the top like icing. This was surprising, since unlike Americans, the Vietnamese usually didn't eat cakes or sweets.

As we finished the meal, the children started returning to their homes after school ended for the day. Many of them carried a small stack of very thin books. Most of the girls were dressed in long pants and white or light-colored shirts with long sleeves. The boys dressed in shorts and white or light-colored shirts with short sleeves. The boys stopped to talk with us and ask about candy that we might share. The girls tended to pass by and continue walking home.

Later in the afternoon several of us went boating in three of the dozen or so sampans that were used by the villagers. The village was located on a river and had a small tributary that ran right through the center of the village. The sampans were extremely swift and even more maneuverable than a canoe. I spent almost two hours going up and down the river. It was a great experience. We finally packed up our gear and left at about 15:30.

We continued to spend most of our time in our base camp or in the field going out on patrols. We didn't get into towns except for an occasional village such as the one I described. I made it to the PX about once every two months.

My family sent me a checklist of foods and snacks that I could request for packages. This made it easier to shop. I liked this checklist idea, since I could identify items that I really enjoyed. When I saw boned chicken on the list I quickly crossed it out. We had boned chicken in our C-rations, and I was sick of it. The deviled ham, however, was one of my favorites. It was a great way to shop, since I couldn't remember all of the varieties available for foods and snacks.

We started getting the camp ready for another move. Rumor now had it that we would be setting up in a camp located just outside of Saigon near Tan Son Nhut Air Base, a real groovy place to be, come Tet. I wasn't too concerned. Having grown up in Brooklyn, I was accustomed to street fighting.

We were out on a sweep and had another interesting day. Moving through some tall grass, I was the last man in the file. We were blowing up some VC bunkers that we had discovered while on patrol. The man in front of me moved out but forgot to tell me he was moving. When I noticed the file was gone I started moving forward to catch up. I had gone about one hundred feet when I heard someone yell "Fire in the hole," the standard warning before detonating an explosive. I yelled at the top of my lungs "Where?" The man with the detonator stood up and said that I was about ten feet from the charge. I moved out smartly, got down, and they blew the bunker. It was close, but I guess that somebody happened to be looking out for me at that moment.

Later in the day I had an experience that was straight out of a Charlie Chaplin movie. We were crossing a small stream about seven feet wide. There was a log lying across the stream, and everyone was using it as a bridge. Nine men in the file had gone across in front of me without mishap. I was halfway across when the log cracked in half. I landed in water up to my neck. The biggest injury was to my pride, so I crawled out of the stream and up the bank to rejoin the rest of the group. Things improved a bit when we came across a sugar cane field, and I cut off a piece of the raw cane. It was sweet and tasty. You could chew it like celery to get the juice out then spit out the fiber.

I sent my fiancée a note requesting a plastic bubblegum machine with several boxes of bubblegum balls and a box of metal washers to use as slugs. We had been told that we would be going through villages in the near future on pacification projects. I thought the kids would enjoy playing with the bubblegum machine.

We did not move on Monday, November 25, as planned. Part of the reason for the delay might have been the expectation of increased enemy action. Every company in the battalion had contact that day. The VC shot at a couple of choppers and hit one of the door gunners. One company caught a POW, and our company found a weapons cache about four hundred meters from our camp at the edge of a nearby river. It was one of the busiest days in a while.

We received a couple of celebrity visitors that same afternoon. It was definitely a memorable experience when Joey Bishop and Tippi Hedren landed in separate choppers in our base camp as part of a USO tour of the boonies. We had no advance notice of their visit, so it was a real surprise when they showed up. I happened to be in the camp at the time, so I was able to grab my camera and follow them as they walked around, shaking hands with our soldiers and making jokes.

Joey Bishop, the comedian and actor, looked older than I remembered from his TV appearances, but he was eager to meet us and happy to pose for photos. He asked about our home towns and made jokes about the food. I noticed that he wanted to climb to the top of our guard tower, so I went ahead and climbed to the top and took pictures of him as he worked his way up the ladder. He posed next to the man who was on guard duty and then used binoculars to survey the area.

Tippi Hedren, actress and mother of four, seemed a bit nervous, but smiled and also posed for pictures with any GIs who wanted to have a picture taken. Most of us remembered her as the star in Alfred Hitchcock's *The Birds*. She wore white pants and a bright-red shirt decorated with the pins and emblems of the different units that she had visited while on this tour. One of our men gave her a puppy that was the mascot of one of the platoons. She enjoyed holding the dog and chatting with our guys.

About half an hour after they arrived, one of the infantry platoons came back through the wire from a long patrol. Joey Bishop headed over to the wire and stopped to say hello and shake hands with each soldier as he came through. They had obviously crossed a couple of rivers, because many were still soaking wet up to their shirts. They enjoyed the unexpected welcome, although some were a bit bewildered by this unusual set of visitors.

Joey Bishop, TV and movie
star, visits our camp.

Tippi Hedren, star of *The
Birds*, poses with author.

Joey Bishop climbs to the top of the guard tower to get a better view of the camp.

After spending an hour at our camp, Joey and Tippi headed to their respective choppers and took off for some other base camp. Most of us never saw Bob Hope when he visited Vietnam, but we did have this opportunity for a celebrity sighting. It was a day that most of us would remember for a long time.

We spent the rest of the evening packing up all of our gear and weapons as we got ready for the move that was now definite.

# CHAPTER 10

# FORT APACHE

On Tuesday, November 26, we moved from the NDP to our new home, Fort Apache, about two miles northeast of Saigon along Highway 1. We spent most of the morning getting ready and at midday, a large Chinook helicopter arrived. Some of our troops got on board carrying most of the gear by hand. Some of the larger items were loaded in two-wheel trailers that were normally pulled by jeeps or trucks. It took six men to pull and push these trailers up the load ramp of the Chinook. It was a short flight to the landing site at the water plant where trucks were waiting for us. We climbed on and were driven to our new camp. In the center of the compound stood a tall flagpole. At the top flew an American flag on one side and a South Vietnamese flag on the other.

The jets that came into Tan Son Nhut Air Base flew right over our heads. The camp itself was pretty miserable. The whole company was crammed into three buildings that looked like long barracks. We had a platoon and a half living in each shed. The barracks were comprised of rough wooden frames resting on cement slabs. Corrugated-metal panels covered the sides and roof. The double-deck bunks were two feet apart, causing everyone to step all over each other. I opted for an upper bunk, hoping to catch a bit more breeze on warm evenings. Sandbags were stacked about three feet high around the sides of the building, providing some protection from any incoming rifle rounds for those on the lower bunks. During our stay there, we gradually raised the height of the sandbag walls. Initially, I hated the place. Inside the perimeter wire, roughly the area of half a city block, there was not a lot of space to expand.

A smaller unit had previously occupied this base camp. Our mission was to build up the defenses of this position, while we continued with our usual patrols. We were told we'd be going out the following day and every day after that to a nearby village on a pacification project. Pacification meant helping the villagers, with the hope that they would remain loyal to the South Vietnamese government. Our duties included providing medical services and passing out candy to the kids. Our presence provided implied support and protection from possible attack. This was to be a welcome change of pace from the endless sweeps in the boonies.

At the base camp, our first duty was to set up the mortars in the three existing mortar pits. The aiming stakes were set in place, and mortar rounds were stacked, ready to go when needed. The next few days we filled sandbags (between patrols) used to protect existing structures and to build new bunkers. The camp was laid out in the form of a rough rectangle. One short side of the rectangle faced an open field that was the most likely path of an attack. This side had the heaviest concentration of bunkers. At each corner there was a large two-story bunker. Three other bunkers were built between the two corners and spaced closely together. All of the bunkers featured two wooden firing ports. These wood-framed apertures opened out to the field, allowing soldiers to fire out with a high degree of protection. The ports were about fifteen inches tall and two feet wide. One covered the frontal position and part of the left flank. The other also covered the frontal position and part of the right flank. This arrangement allowed for overlapping fields of fire.

There was a permanent guard with the M-2 .50-caliber machine gun stationed on top of one of the corner bunkers. Another permanent guard armed with his M-16 and an M-67 recoilless rifle sat on top of the other corner bunker. The M-67 is similar to a bazooka in the way that it is fired. We did not anticipate any enemy tanks in this area of operation, so the guard had a stack of antipersonnel rounds next to him. When these were fired, they exploded on impact and released pieces of flying metal. The only other time that I had seen this weapon in Vietnam was at the water plant where a couple of these were mounted on jeeps. We normally carried a different weapon when out on patrols, the M-72 LAW. The LAW was a five pound antitank weapon, only two feet long and easy to carry. It was used against enemy machine gun positions or to fire into a tight clump of trees, where the enemy might be hiding.

We built the new bunkers with sandbags that were stacked tightly to form four walls, which were topped with six-by-six timbers to form a square. The roof was covered with a layer of thick wood planks nailed down with thick spikes. The planks were then covered with two or three layers of sandbags.

When these bunkers were completed, they served two functions since they were firing positions but were also used as hootches to help relieve the overcrowding in the barracks. They provided a high degree of protection from rifle rounds as well as mortar and rocket shrapnel. There was no guarantee of survival from a direct hit with a mortar or rocket round, but we all understood that Vietnam was a risky place to work. If a hootch could provide protection for 90 percent of the probable dangers we might encounter, we were very satisfied with that margin of safety.

A short dirt road lined with concertina wire led from our camp to a wooden gate and a small guardhouse that faced the main road. A permanent guard was posted at this gate. The local Vietnamese vendors were aware that we entered and exited this camp at different times during the day. One or two young boys usually showed up in the early morning and remained by the roadside until late afternoon, selling sodas from plastic coolers. The main road was moderately busy, with a number of motorbikes and Lambrettas as well as ARVN and US Army trucks and jeeps traveling the road daily. The road led to Saigon in one direction and to the town of Thu Duc in the other.

Children in a village we visited as part of the pacification program.

Our first day at Fort Apache, setting up the mortars and trying to find space for our gear in the crowded barracks.

We were now just two months away from Tet 1969, the Lunar New Year, and a major holiday in Vietnam. Everyone was concerned about a repeat of the 1968 Tet Offensive which began on January 30 and continued into February and March. There was a sense of urgency in the buildup of defenses at Fort Apache and at camps all over Vietnam. The entire 18th Infantry Brigade was under orders to reinforce all positions. The new bunkers we built were located close to our perimeter, including some facing the nearby road, likely places of attack.

There was some evidence that hostile action had already taken place nearby. Along the highway that passed near Fort Apache, a few hundred meters from our camp, a large metal billboard advertised "Mac Phsu," some type of medical balm or ointment. The sign was perforated with bullet holes. It was a constant reminder that we were in hostile territory.

Mail call brought some good news. I received a package from home that was full of snack items and an assortment of Christmas decorations. We planned to use the decorations to set up a small artificial tree in the barracks.

Two days after our arrival, it was Thanksgiving Day. It started with a patrol to a nearby village. The village (about a mile in length) was located on both sides of a highway. To get there we had to cross a couple of rice paddies, soaking our boots and fatigues in the process. I thought to myself that back home it was Thanksgiving Day, and everyone was eating multicourse dinners with family and friends. I was on patrol, however, without even a lousy stick of gum. It rained in the afternoon and made the day even more miserable.

When we returned to the camp, we found that our bunks had been rearranged, and our gear was moved in every direction. We had to search out our gear and set it up again. Then we went to the mess hall for our Thanksgiving dinner.

Each soldier received a small printed menu that started with a prayer. "Our gracious Father, whose power and Deity is apparent through the things that are made, hear our prayer. We thank Thee for the love which we share with family and friends, which prompts us to call the stranger, neighbor. We thank Thee for health and sound bodies, whereby we may serve Thee, our country and others. We thank Thee for the United States and for all that is right and noble in her past and present. We thank Thee for a world in which the voices of honorable and wise men can still be heard. Above all, our Father, we thank Thee for Thyself. In our pause to give thanks, we are again reminded that we are debtors indeed. Lead our nation by leading each of us in Thy service. For Thy kingdom's sake. Amen." The prayer was written by Chaplain (Col) Gerard J. Gefell.

The cooks made a special effort to prepare a delicious meal, and there was a good selection of food including shrimp cocktail, roast turkey, cornbread dressing, gravy, cranberry sauce, mashed potatoes, glazed sweet potatoes, mixed vegetables, assorted crisp relishes, hot rolls with butter, fruitcake, mincemeat pie, pumpkin pie, assorted nuts, candy, fresh fruits, and iced tea with lemon or milk.

I was recalling those TV and radio announcements back in the States reminding people to "...pause for a moment to think about our boys in Vietnam." I was glad everyone paused for a minute. I also paused for a minute, and I don't have to tell you on which side of the Pacific I'd have preferred to be during that particular moment. After dinner I walked around the compound and caught sight of the pet monkey that had shown up at our NDP. He had managed to come with us to Fort Apache but had been lying low to avoid detection. Several guys smiled at the sight of the monkey. It was nice to see an old friend.

The day ended on a pragmatic note. I had bunker guard duty from midnight to 06:00, and we were going out again the next day. On the bright side, that day marked five months in Vietnam, so I was getting closer to the halfway mark.

It turned out that we did not go out on a patrol on Friday, but I was assigned guard duty at the gate leading to the main highway. The large wood-frame gate was covered with barbed wire. Trucks and jeeps drove in and out of our camp. Outside the gate, a couple of mama-sans with babies sold beer, plastic hammocks, mirrors, and other assorted items.

The portable television set that I mentioned earlier belonged to the first sergeant, and he turned it on every evening. Usually, I was too tired or too busy writing letters, but I watched maybe one show a week. The commercials were a little different. Instead of selling a product, they reminded us to take our malaria pills, use insect repellent, keep our ammo clean, etc. Morale levels in the unit varied by day, but it was generally good. I was starting to get used to the place.

Christina mentioned in a letter that something was on its way in the mail that should "last and last." I guessed that it was a fruitcake. I had talked to the guys who were there last year, and it seemed everyone received at least one or two fruitcakes. They said there was so much fruitcake around that you couldn't even give it away to the Vietnamese.

After our arrival we were engaged in a major construction program, building bunkers, pouring a cement floor for the mess hall, and building latrines. The additional bunkers were to serve two functions. They provided additional secure firing positions in case of attack, and they also provided extra living space to relieve overcrowding in the barracks buildings. Another change was the modification of manpower for patrols. Two of the platoons went out on ambush every night, and the other two platoons went on sweeps during the day. That way we had more men available for all of the construction projects. We continued building for the next couple of weeks until the camp was really well fortified. I had bunker guard duty almost every night.

As the holidays grew closer, I sent Christmas cards to my family, my fiancée, and some close relatives and friends. The card was a photo of me taken a few weeks earlier with a preprinted message, "Merry Christmas, Happy New Year" with a drawing of a horse and sleigh in the snow. On the back I wrote to my family, "I don't think I'll be seeing any snow this year, but it will be my last year in the army, so I think I can make it. By the time you get this, I'll have less than six months left in the army. I'm starting to get *short*! Have a happy holiday."

In her Christmas letter, Christina sent me a picture of her wearing a beautiful new pink dress. One of our Vietnamese interpreters was looking at it and said that he thought she looked like a real doll. His exact words were "Number one, number one!" which is high praise indeed, since number one is perfect, but number ten is terrible.

Christina also told me that her adoption agency had just placed its five-thousandth baby, a major milestone for her and the agency.

My new rank as sergeant hadn't changed my duties much at this point, but I did receive a raise and now had certain privileges. I could now go to the NCO club and have a few drinks. On paper, I no longer had to pull KP, guard duty, or other menial jobs. Instead, I'd be in charge of those jobs. There were only two problems with those privileges. The first was that with the exception of KP (which only the cooks pull), we did have guard duty, and we did perform menial tasks. The "normal" rules only applied in fully staffed units stateside. The second problem was that, while it's great to be able to go to the NCO club, there were no NCO clubs in the compound. The bigger changes would occur in January or February when most of the current sergeants in our company finished their tours and left Vietnam.

One of our men purchased a brand-new radio at the PX that was capable of picking up faraway signals. One day he was scanning different frequencies and for a few minutes was able to pick up WABC radio from New York City. It was the Dan Ingram show, which was very popular in the New York metro area at the time. I could hardly believe my ears. There was a lot of static, but I recognized his voice. I felt a little closer to home.

In the evening, it was our platoon's turn to stay in the camp, so two other platoons went out on an ambush. They were setting up in their position when the VC surprised them and started firing rifles and rocket-propelled grenades. We had one man slightly wounded with shrapnel. The company returned fire and wound up killing two VC and capturing one alive. The men who were on this mission, said that it was a very intense firefight. They were glad to return to camp in the morning.

On Wednesday, December 4, I was finally able to ride the supply truck to the main base in Di An and had the opportunity to make my first MARS call. It was great to hear my mother's voice and to talk to my brother Gary.

A MARS call (military affiliated radio service) was a system of radio relays combining military and "ham" radio operators. The radio relay went as close as possible to the town you wanted to call. In my case I think the ham operator was in New York, although he could have been in California. The last radio in the hookup connects with a telephone, where he dials the number you are calling.

You can talk both ways at once on a telephone, but on a radio the sound goes in one direction at a time. On a given frequency, only one set can transmit at a time while the other sets are receiving. To communicate, each party takes turns transmitting. Military and ham radios were combination receivers and transmitters; so, when the stateside party was talking, the radio operator at the other end of their phone line was transmitting to other radio operators back to Vietnam. The radio operator at my end was receiving. When they said "over" it indicated that they were finished talking. When I started talking, the US radio operator then put his set on receive, and the Vietnam radio operator put his set on transmit. There was a three-minute time limit for calls. The call was free up to the point where it reached a ham operator in the United States. I would then pay for normal call charges from that location to my family's phone.

The nearest place that had a MARS station was at Di An, and I only got there once every two months or so. It usually took six to twelve hours to get a time slot for a call. I'd put my name on a list and wait. Luckily, my slot was available in just ten minutes, since I only had three hours before I had to get back to my camp. I told my folks that I received the Christmas tree and the decorations and hoped that everything was OK with them. I really enjoyed hearing their voices.

Someone asked me about personal mistakes or bad luck and yes, I had made a couple of mistakes. The worst one occurred when I reconned an ambush site. I had located a nice dry berm that was about two feet higher than the rest of the ground around it. There was only two inches of water in the field so I figured that we could return at night, set up on the berm and cover an ambush of the river that was a few meters to our front. We returned that night with a patrol of about thirty-five men. It was dark, and I was using my compass to find the site. I had just started across the last field before reaching the berm when I began to realize that something was wrong. The water that had been two inches high in the afternoon was now up to my chest. When we reached the berm, it was under a foot and a half of water. I had quite a bit of egg on my face as thirty-five waterlogged (and highly pissed off) men moved back three hundred meters to a dryer spot farther up river.

We built a platform for the two water trailers used at our new camp. It was constructed with timbers and gravel that were shipped in by the engineer corps. We now got our water on trailers that were towed back and forth to Di An, where they were refilled. Our proximity to the highway also made it convenient to use trucks to transport the rest of our food, ammo, supplies, and laundry.

Our mortar platoon continued to fill sandbags and build bunkers through the first week of December, while the three other infantry platoons went out on missions. We needed to stay back to provide rapid mortar support when needed. Even though the calendar said December, we felt the weather getting warmer as the cooling rains came to an end.

We decided to make our barracks look more like home with the Christmas decorations we had been receiving from our families. We set up the artificial tree and other decorations at one end of the room. Someone took spare bulbs used for our flashlights, wired them together, and then connected the wire to one of the larger radio batteries. We hung these on the small tree. Each light was backed with colored foil. We added silver tinsel and lit up the tree every evening until Christmas. Under the tree we even placed a small stack of presents that had been arriving from our families.

I received a large package from Christina that included a box of chocolate chip cookies and a fruitcake. Contrary to the conventional humor regarding fruitcakes, this one was delicious, with large chunks of fruit and nuts. It was also infused with lots of whiskey, so it was well preserved and held up well on the trip over. She also sent a gold metallic holiday decoration with a starburst design. We placed it on top of the Christmas tree that we had set up in the barracks. It looked great! The tree lifted our spirits and helped us keep pace with the rest of the world.

On Monday, December 9, we heard that there were two NVA (North Vietnamese army) divisions heading toward Saigon. It was reported in *Time, Newsweek,* and *US News & World Report.* Among the GIs, there were also rumors of large masses of troops in and around Saigon and across the border in Cambodia. It looked as if a major battle was shaping up.

That day they asked for volunteers to transfer to the 1st Air Cavalry Division, which had recently come down from up north. I declined. I preferred to stay with the Big Red One and the unit where I had already spent five months patrolling in the rice paddies and jungles of the delta region.

Some of the men in our company seriously thought about transferring to the 1st Air Cav. Possibly, the continual sweeps with little direct contact was getting to them. The basic routine was boring and monotonous at times, but I had been pretty lucky so far. The army was not going to be a permanent career path for me. I respected the men I worked with and did not want to start a new learning curve in another unit. I didn't know what lay ahead in the next seven months in terms of combat. With the 1st Air Cav, there may have been more opportunity for larger scale battles, which would have meant more advancement and better pay but also higher risks.

During the second week of December, we joined the other infantry platoon on patrols. We rotated the patrols so that there was always at least one platoon left behind to defend the camp. Our mission changed a bit as we placed more emphasis on pacification and spent time visiting villages. It was a two-pronged approach. We spent part of the time looking for VC in the fields and rice paddies and the rest of the time visiting villages to reassure them that we would support them and be close by to protect them from the Viet Cong. The fact that some of these villages may have harbored VC made the task difficult. We tried to make the best of it and generally got a welcome reception in most of the villages with little or no open hostility. Much of this may have been due to geography. Our proximity to Saigon meant there were large concentrations of American and South Vietnamese troops ready to defend and protect the capital. Soldiers in other areas of the country faced stronger opposition and a great deal of hostility in many of the rural villages.

Wednesday, December 11, started out as a good day. I hit the halfway mark and had exactly six months left. I would be getting shorter with each passing day. The Red Cross volunteers stopped by our camp again, passing out books, etc. I also received an audiotape from Christina and was able to play it on a buddy's tape player. It was a great morale booster to hear her voice.

Then I heard some discouraging news about our location. It was formerly an ARVN compound that had been overrun by the Viet Cong the previous February. I assumed that this was the primary reason we were building up and fortifying this position. We were pretty well equipped, with three mortars, two .50-caliber guns, plus our normal machine guns, rifles, etc. The rumors continued to persist about the two NVA divisions and assorted smaller elements heading toward Saigon. Our compound was supposedly in their path.

That night we were on yellow alert, with all bunkers manned, and everyone sleeping with his weapon. A yellow alert meant that there was a better than fifty-fifty chance of contact. I had to sleep in one of the mortar pits so that we were in a position to respond rapidly. I pulled a poncho around me, tried to find a comfortable position in the pit, and eventually fell asleep. At 03:00 we awoke to the firing of a machine gun. I jumped up, grabbed my helmet, and put on my flak jacket. It turned that one of our guys was firing at a shadow. There was nothing out there. Everyone was a bit jumpy.

In the morning we set out on a long patrol to a village. We were moving on foot the whole day and had to cover ten klicks each way. Things were quiet in the village, and we returned without incident. We repeated this cycle for the next few days.

We went through the same village for the third day in a row and then continued past that village quite a distance until we were in rice paddies, mud, and swamps again. As we came back through the village, we spent time talking with the villagers and passing out candy to the kids. It was a pretty good day. We planned to go to a different village the next day, but with the same pacification objective. This type of mission was more interesting for me, because we had the opportunity to interact with the locals and learn a little more about their way of life.

We continued to go out on long patrols every day, and I had bunker guard duty every night. I was feeling exhausted, but no one ever said that army life was easy or fun. On the bright side, I did receive confirmation that my R&R request had come through, and I would be going to Sydney, Australia, from January 26 to February 2. This was great news. Also, Christina confirmed that she had shipped the bubblegum machine I had requested and that it should be arriving soon. I was sure that the children in the villages we were visiting would get a kick out of this.

In the meantime, the daily routine was starting to wear everyone down. The platoon started to develop a morale problem. We were short on men, and everyone was getting extremely tired and edgy from the repeated hikes to villages during the day and high-alert guard duty at night. Those were long exhausting days.

Finally, we received a brief break. Instead of a day in the field, we stayed in the camp and filled sandbags. One of the other platoons, however, headed out on a night ambush, and just as they were moving into position, they were hit. One man was wounded in the shoulder and was dusted off. Ironically, while the peace talks were underway in Paris, things hadn't changed very much for us on the ground.

Friday, December 20, started out with some better news. Four new replacements joined our platoon, so things were bound to get better. For me, there would be no more bunker guard duty. I also received a batch of almost two thousand black-and-white prints from the photo shop at Di An. It would take me a couple of days to sort out and distribute them to the men in our company. They wanted to send them home to their families and friends before Christmas.

The day that started out so well ended badly. That night one of the men in our platoon was seriously hurt. Three of our men were assigned to bridge detail every night. The purpose of the mission was to watch for flashes from mortar or rocket launchers and then call in the compass direction and estimated distance to headquarters. These guys decided to go diving into the river from the bridge. One man climbed up on one of the bridge towers to dive off and may have lost his balance. He reached out for a wire to catch himself. The wire was a live power line. He got a severe shock and was thrown twenty-five to thirty feet to the roadway of the bridge. They took him to the main hospital in Saigon in critical condition.

Shortly after, there was another incident. One of our platoons had set up in an ambush position. A VC walked up on the rear position. One of our men saw him and opened fire. The VC, who had mistakenly walked in between two of our positions, turned and started firing. He shot four GIs before he was killed. Our men who were firing at him shot two more GIs who were behind the VC. All of our wounded men survived, although some of them would be hospitalized for several months. Some were sent home to the States. It was a bad night.

The next day there was a big shakeup in the company. The man who had fallen from the bridge was still alive but severely injured. He had both legs and one arm amputated, had permanent brain damage, and was still in critical condition. He was moved to a hospital in Japan. War seems like a damned waste of men and talent much of the time, but this event was particularly foolish and senseless.

The other two men who were on the bridge detail were taken off that assignment and attached to the platoon that went out on ambushes every night. One of them was eventually court-martialed with only eighteen days left in-country. The four new guys were sent to the ambush platoon to replace the six wounded men.

The next day we headed out on a new village patrol. A sniper began shooting at us as we were getting ready to check some of the dwellings. We maneuvered around and started closing in on his position. I went with another man to check one hootch. The river had risen with the tide, higher than normal, and there was a foot of water on the ground. As I sloshed through the water toward the house, I lost my balance and fell into a watery ditch that was five feet deep. I climbed out, and we continued moving forward. We rushed into the house from opposite sides with a finger on the trigger only to find an old woman calmly cooking some rice and fish. The sniper had escaped. Once again, an elusive enemy had evaded us.

Our platoon sergeant left for an R&R in Taipei. The second squad leader was now the acting platoon sergeant, and I was the acting squad leader for the second squad. I was busier now, but it was more interesting. On my first day as squad leader, we went out on patrols to nearby villages. Everything went well, and it turned out to be a quiet day.

We heard the news that they released the crewmen from the Pueblo that same day. It appeared that the United States had really messed up that operation.

# CHAPTER 11

# CHRISTMAS IN VIETNAM

It was Christmas Eve. Our small tree was brightly lit, the mini-stockings were on the makeshift mantel, and presents from our families were under the tree. A Christmas truce was in effect for twenty-four hours. Big deal! We had two different ambush positions out that night, and another patrol was going out the following day. If there was contact with the Viet Cong, we were waiting to see who opened up first.

It was a strange night. Christmas carols were playing on personal radios throughout the base. Everyone would rather have been someplace other than this camp. We were quietly thankful that there had been no contact that day, and we hoped it would continue that way for at least one more day.

Christmas Day dawned quietly and peacefully. We kept busy in the early part of the day, but everything seemed to lighten up in the afternoon, except for those on guard duty. I took time to open a couple of packages from home that I had been saving for Christmas. I received a nice assortment of homemade cookies and snacks. I also received some lens filters I had requested for my camera. I was concerned that they might be the wrong size or color, but they both fit my camera perfectly.

We enjoyed a delicious Christmas dinner similar to the Thanksgiving feast. It was welcomed and appreciated by everyone. We tried to get in the Christmas spirit. There was some horseplay and good-natured kidding around, but there was no escaping the reality that we were in a war zone and far from home. While some people may have missed a Christmas at home before, today was the first time that most of us had been this far away on this particular holiday. We didn't spend too much time dwelling on these thoughts. Most of us were still exhausted by the constant physical demands of patrols, ambushes, guard duty, and defensive construction. If we had some free time, we'd write a couple of quick letters, read, or listen to music. We didn't stay up late, because we knew there was another mission tomorrow, and we'd be going out whether we felt rested or not.

I told my family not to look for me on TV during the *Bob Hope Special*. We didn't make it to the show. Our routine as a mortar platoon had changed since we arrived at Fort Apache. Our role now was to support the other platoons with mortar fire if needed, so we no longer went out on night ambushes. The ambush sites were pretty close to our camp, so I wasn't required to go out as the FO with them. I did start going out with the bridge detail, spending the night watching for rocket flashes. It was known as the Go Dua Bridge on the road to Thu Duc. During the day we continued the pacification projects and patrols and would operate like this for the next month and a half.

Our platoon had been visiting two villages on a pretty regular basis. They were getting to know us, and we were getting to know them. We passed out candy and C-rations, and the medics performed simple first aid and handed out aspirin, antibiotics, etc.

On Friday, December 27, I was back on the bridge detail and getting into the routine of the job. We alternated the watches at night, so we were all able to get some sleep.

We had a much needed stand-down the following day. Two Red Cross volunteers visited us and spent a couple of hours smiling and talking with the guys in our platoon. I later learned that a total of 627 young women had volunteered to improve the morale of soldiers in Vietnam by participating in the Supplemental Recreational Activities Overseas (SRAO) program of the Red Cross. They were all college graduates who had agreed to spend a year in the program. They were sometimes referred to by their nickname, which was "Donut Dollies," but we didn't see many donuts in our smaller camps, so we just called them the Red Cross Girls.

The medics came around after they left and gave out shots and booster shots. I made sure I had all the shots I would need for Australia. I received two booster shots for cholera and plague. My left arm was sore as hell, but I'd be ready to go next month on my R&R.

After their visit, I realized how much I missed talking to a woman. The separation from Christina was difficult, and I was reluctant to check the calendar, since I still had a long time left in Vietnam. The day ended well, with two great letters from Christina and a package containing some snacks and a few pairs of dry socks, among other things. The socks were definitely a welcome gift, since supply still had trouble keeping them in stock.

We went out to the village again the next day and went through our usual friendly pacification routine. At night I was on bridge guard again. I hadn't taken a shower or shaved in two days. I talked with the first sergeant, and he said that our platoon was scheduled to get more men soon, so we'd have an opportunity for an occasional stand-down.

We also heard that Apollo 8 splashed down safely the previous night after completing a lunar orbit, and everything was A-OK with that project. The three-man crew, Frank Borman, James Lovell, and William Anders, were the first humans to see the far side of the moon and succeeded in making ten orbits of the moon. It was good to hear about a success for the United States.

A Red Cross volunteer visits Fort Apache, spending time socializing with men in our unit. They were part of the SRAO (Supplemental Recreation Activities Overseas) program to boost morale.

We spent Monday, December 30, providing security while one of the villages built a bridge over a small stream with materials we supplied. It seemed like a more equitable program, with the Vietnamese providing the labor rather than having us build it for them. They did seem to appreciate the security and the new bridge, which would enable them to access their rice paddies and fields more easily.

My fiancée mentioned that the village children in many of my photos looked healthy and did not appear to be starving as a result of the war. I explained that these children were well fed and generally pretty healthy. South Vietnam was important to the communists for its abundance of food. Some felt that South Vietnam had the potential to provide enough rice to feed every person in Asia.

In addition to rice, there were fairly abundant supplies of grapefruit, pineapple, and various other fruits growing in the country. If the children wanted candy (when they weren't eating the items that the GIs were passing out) they would cut a stalk of sugar cane and chew it. The fresh sugar cane was cool, sweet, and juicy.

It was New Year's Eve on the last Tuesday in 1968. I was on the bridge again, feeling fatigued since we'd been going day and night. The New Year was to start in five minutes, and my flashlight wasn't going to last, so I tried to quickly finish a letter to Christina. I told her that I was sorry I couldn't be with her, but I believed that 1969 was going to be a happier year for us. I ended with "Happy New Year!"

We celebrated on the bridge eating cookies and drinking lemonade. I was spending the nights on this bridge with a couple of other guys on a shift that lasted from 18:00 to 06:00. The bridge itself was guarded by a company of ARVNs who lived in the twenty or so bunkers on both sides of the bridge and on the bridge itself. The ARVN who was sitting next to me on the bridge was sixteen, had no parents, and had been in the army over a year. He said he had already personally killed seven VC. It was a different world over there.

Once again we felt a little depressed about our situation. We were standing guard while much of the world whooped it up with friends, drinks, and music. If we had not made a commitment to complete our tour of service, none of us on the bridge, American or ARVN, would have chosen to stay there. For most Americans, this was a one-year commitment, although some would choose to return for a second tour. However, the Vietnamese were in it for the "duration," much as American troops were during World War II. This night passed quietly, the sun rose, and we headed back to Fort Apache. A new year had begun. This would turn out to be perhaps the most significant year of my life. I didn't dwell on it at the time; I was simply trying to get through one more day.

## 1969, A New Year

As January unfolded, we continued the routine of pacifying villages during the day and standing watch on the bridge at night.

One of the men who had been diving off the bridge when the soldier was injured was walking around with a chip on his shoulder ever since the accident. He thought that everyone blamed him for being on top of that bridge and causing the accident. As a matter of fact, no one had said anything to him except the company commander. He tried to start a fight with me several times. We had two run-ins, and he took a light swing at me twice. The first time wasn't too bad, but the second time, I almost had it out with him. We were fairly evenly matched in size, and I believed that I would have beaten him. But I was an NCO. If I was involved in a brawl, the consequences for me were worse than the enlisted man, unless I could prove it was self-defense. I didn't like the situation and hoped he'd cool off. Eventually, after a couple of weeks things calmed down. I guess time heals all wounds, physical and psychological.

We spent Saturday, January 4, building a hootch for one of the squads in our platoon. We were continuing to build four of these structures so that some men could move out of the barracks and provide more room for everyone. I was really tiring of the place.

Filling sandbags during the day and sitting on a bridge at night was not the most interesting work in the world.

We spent most of the next day digging up a field near a spot where they had recently found a tunnel complex and several VC. We found nothing.

On Monday morning, after spending the night on the bridge, I woke up from a sound sleep to a loud roaring noise. When I opened my eyes I saw an eighty-ton locomotive roaring by about eighteen inches from my head. We were on a double bridge with a train trestle on the left and a highway on the right. We slept on a bunker that was right next to the tracks. I usually left my gear on the tracks, but that night I had tossed the stuff on the bunker. Glad I did. It was the first time that I had seen a train on those tracks.

I received a wedding announcement from a close friend from college. I could not attend the wedding, but I planned to send him a gift. I was lucky the next day and made it into Di An on the supply truck. It was very difficult finding him a suitable wedding gift. The PX was closing for several days of inventory, and the stock was very low. I purchased a set of three large photo albums and airmailed them to him.

We spent most of the day filling sandbags again, before heading out to the bridge in the evening. It was very quiet and peaceful on the bridge and I was feeling a bit down. I spent several hours writing a poem with glimpses of some of my recent experiences. Some of it was inspired by my friend's wedding announcement and the conflicting emotions of a calmer stateside life compared to the daily challenges I was facing. I had reached the halfway point of my tour in Vietnam, but still had six more months to go and my departure date seemed a very long way off. Here is the poem.

## AFTER SIX MONTHS

A body, buddy is dragged from the river,
You grab his tongue and grasp for the life that is gone.
A slick leaves you, wet and lonely.
You sit and watch, for the kid who is sitting and watching.
He climbs to dive for life; with a snap crackle falls to numbness,
You pity, frustrate, infuriate.
Picture a boy and his dog; the picture's the whole, the boy is the half,
You smile at a woman, smiling at her husband.
A twelve-toed boy asks for chop-chop,
You half-laugh, "No sweat, baby-san," and he turns to the next.
A warm bowl, rice and fish, at one in the morning, (smile),
"You get me radio?"
"Pacify the civilians!!!"...Please?
You chide, plead, admonish.
A shadow moves, an AK rings,
And final score is tallied,
You have two and we have won and four errors.
A cloud floats by, the weeds flow free,
You are or you aren't! Yes.
The announcement is received, with love and yes
They each will marry,
You think, it's been a long time.

We continued our pacification visits to a nearby village and were generally welcomed by the children and the adults. I brought the bright-yellow plastic bubblegum machine with me, and it was an immediate hit. I had a supply of plastic discs that served as coin substitutes, since it was designed to be used as a kid's bank. The boys understood how the machine worked and politely took turns dispensing the colored gum balls. They watched intently as each one inserted a plastic disc and pushed the lever to get a gum ball. We expected it to be a quiet mission that day, so I brought my camera and got several great images of the children, fascinated by this toy. Eventually, the small crowd of boys opened up to allow some of the girls to try the machine. They all had a great time.

After an hour, the machine was empty. I packed it away and promised that I would return in a couple of weeks with a new supply of gum balls. They headed off with their friends. Some of them found a tall palm tree with multiple branches providing good footholds as they climbed. They took turns showing off as each one inched a little higher than the previous one. At one point there were three boys in the tree and a fourth trying to make his way to the top.

Another group of boys found a flat spot in the dirt and were playing a game of marbles. Some of them seemed exceptionally skilled at hitting the target marble with a great deal of accuracy. We didn't know if marbles had a worldwide following, or if they'd received bags of marbles from an earlier group of GIs. In any case, they seemed to enjoy the competition, and some of the boys walked off with a larger bag than they started with.

One of the members of our platoon found a large green coconut under a tree and used his machete to cut away the outer husk to reach the center and enjoy the sweet liquid inside.

Boys enjoy the bubblegum machine.

Vendors sell fresh produce in the village market.

We came across coconuts frequently during our stay in Vietnam, but we didn't usually have the time to cut them up, because we took very short breaks and needed to keep the noise level low. The pacification visits allowed us to spend a little more time with the people and also sample the coconuts and sugar cane that we found.

Everyone enjoyed the pacification missions, because we had a good track record of peaceful visits without being fired on while in these villages. Once again, this was probably due to our proximity to Saigon. We heard that other units had different experiences in other areas of the country, especially in the north in I Corps. That morning's visit to the village came to an abrupt end, and we headed out on a new mission.

Along the side of the road, we passed a nice-looking house with stucco walls, rather than the thatched bamboo we had seen in many of the poorer villages. Nailed to a tree in front of the house was a large metal sign depicting a ferocious German shepherd with its mouth open, showing large fang-like teeth and a long tongue. The sign warned in French, "Attention Chien Mechant," (Beware of the Vicious Dog). We didn't see or hear any dogs. We checked the back and the front of the house. The door was locked, and no one appeared to be home. Since this house was in the area we were trying to pacify, we did not make any further efforts to enter the house.

We continued walking along a paved road on our way back to camp. We passed a civilian bus that had been stopped by a local South Vietnamese policeman. It was a routine check. He was wearing a white shirt with short sleeves, khaki pants, and a revolver in the holster hanging from his belt. He checked the papers of the driver then moved back along the bus to examine each of the passengers. Most of the passengers were women and a few old men. The passengers appeared familiar with security checks like this and didn't seem to be alarmed.

While the policeman checked the bus moving from the front gradually to the rear, a female vendor carrying plates of fruit and chunks of sugar cane worked her way along the side of the bus moving from the back to the front selling her snacks. The policeman completed his ID checks at the back of the bus just as she finished her last sale at the front. Once again the choreography of life in Vietnam played out in a daily ballet.

Farther down the road we saw two Vietnamese civilian workers in a large yellow "cherry picker," installing glass insulators at the top of a new wooden utility pole to handle new power lines. It seemed strange to see such an ordinary sight while on patrol looking for Viet Cong. Although it seemed like an impossible task, the South Vietnamese government was trying to expand the infrastructure of the country in the middle of a war. It reminded us of the efforts of President Johnson as he tried to take on two simultaneous projects, waging the war in Vietnam and building the Great Society in the United States.

That night while I was on bridge guard duty, there was an accident unrelated to the war. A woman riding on the back of a motorcycle caught her foot in the spokes of the wheel. Her left foot was smashed up and bleeding. We carried her to our bunker and laid her on a couple of blankets, propped her foot up, and managed to stop the bleeding. We called for a GI medic and an ambulance-jeep, and we treated her for shock. The ambulance finally arrived and took her away. The medic said she would be OK after treatment. We decided that this event was our pacification project for the day.

There was a tall concrete pole cemented into the ground in one corner of our compound. The top of the pole held electric wires from the camp generator, along with a large antenna for communicating with battalion headquarters. Someone in our company figured out a better use for the pole. They fastened a piece of plywood about ten feet off the ground and nailed a basketball hoop to the plywood. Once again, almost magically, a basketball appeared.

Dribbling on the hard dirt that served as a court was a challenge, but it was perfect for practicing shots when we had a free moment (and the ground wasn't muddy). Although the condition of the makeshift court was not ideal, it provided some sense of normalcy in a clearly abnormal situation, a reminder of better times in the past and the hope of better times ahead. We could almost hear the cheers of the crowd at Madison Square Garden as one of the guys sank a great shot.

Long before Christmas I had ordered a stereo set for my family through a listing in a PX catalog. It had not arrived by New Year's Day, but I got a letter on January 10 confirming that it had finally arrived and worked great. My fourteen-year-old brother, Gary, asked me for some kind of war souvenir. We experienced several enemy encounters since arriving in June, but no large scale engagements, which was probably why I was still alive and uninjured. I told him that I didn't have any VC bayonets and that I would have to pay for my bayonet if I sent it to him.

We were not permitted to send or mail any type of automatic weapon, grenade, ammunition, flare, smoke grenade, or star cluster of any kind to the States (used or otherwise). A few years earlier a plane was about to land in San Francisco with a load of guys coming home from Vietnam, when some type of souvenir blew up; they were all killed. Some of these items are pressure sensitive (and dangerous in a pressurized airplane cabin). I promised him I would try to send him a set of ARVN fatigues or some other nonlethal souvenir.

I continued to take pictures whenever I had an opportunity, and the volume of photos was increasing. I felt these visual recordings of my experiences were so valuable that I sent them home for safekeeping.

The next morning we boarded trucks that drove us to a drop-off point for a search and destroy mission. We had an escort consisting of APCs (armored personnel carriers) at the front and rear of our short convoy. The APCs had markings that were now familiar. They were the 1st Squadron 4th US Cavalry, also known by the nicknames 1/4 Horse or Quarter Horse, because they were one of four squadrons. Members of their unit had provided us with an escort numerous times since I had arrived in-country, and they continued to support us for the rest of my tour.

We didn't really know the names of the helicopter units that also provided transportation for us, let alone the names of the pilots or crews. The best that we could do was try to recognize the unit symbol that many painted on their aircraft. During the course of the year, we rode with the Tomahawks (128th Assault Helicopter Company), the Bulldogs (129th Assault Helicopter Company), and other helicopter units that chose not to paint a symbol on their choppers.

We often crossed paths with the men who provided the APC support along with the truck drivers and the helicopter pilots who flew us in and out of the field. We relied on them to show up on time and get us safely to our destinations, yet we barely knew them.

There was little if any verbal communication with the guys in the APCs, and we would be hard-pressed to match a face with a vehicle or aircraft. It was similar to civilian life, where we seldom recognize the face of the bus driver or train engineer who transports us to our place of work. It was hard to know if the APC crews made a difference on the days when they provided an escort and nothing happened. Was there a small group of Viet Cong hiding in the bushes at the side of a lonely road waiting for a target of opportunity? Did the presence of the APCs tip the balance, causing the VC leader to do a quick odds calculation and make the decision not to open fire on us while we were sitting exposed in open trucks? We didn't know the answer, but we were always appreciative for any additional support or protection that we received.

It would be interesting to know the thoughts of the APC crews, truck drivers, and helicopter pilots as well. While they were busy doing their jobs and trying to move us back and forth among different positions, they may have felt that they had the safer job. Infantry is normally the riskiest job in the army, with the highest casualty rates. Perhaps they were happy to drop us off and move back to a safer situation. The reality was that everyone in a combat zone was at risk. The APCs had walls of steel to protect them, but they were sitting ducks if a VC fired an antitank weapon at them. Trucks had very little protection and could easily be ambushed by small arms fire. Helicopters were very vulnerable when they flew close to the ground, as they must when delivering or picking up infantry in the field. In addition, the pilots served two tours, so they placed themselves in danger zones twice as long where they could be wounded or killed.

I wrote a letter in response to Christina's question about the number of men in a platoon. A platoon is supposed to have forty men, but at that time, we had only twenty-three, possibly because there were more guys who wanted to leave here than come here, and Congress was unwilling to send more troops. Every unit needed men; there were never enough as long as the war went on, which might be the best reason to end a war.

She asked if I got any extra pay for night duty. I explained that the army pays us for a twenty-four-hour workday, and any time spent sleeping is considered a waste of time. I asked her not to write my congressman, because there were 499,000 other guys over here with the same problem.

She also asked if I needed clothes for R&R. I explained that all I needed was a clean khaki uniform and a pair of shoes. I had both of these in my footlocker in Di An. They also rented civvies at the R&R center in Australia or sold them at the PX.

We had some unusual excitement the following day. One of the other platoons had almost returned to our NDP when a water buffalo lowered his horns and charged, with no visible provocation whatever. The buffalo was about fifty feet away when it started running. One of the men opened up on full automatic and fired a whole magazine (eighteen rounds) at the buffalo. It finally dropped ten feet in front of the man with the rifle. There was some humor in the situation. At first the buffalo was thought to be a VC suspect, and sure enough, it was later confirmed that he was a fully trained VC. Obviously, he had been hanging around with the wrong herd.

The owner of the buffalo came to Fort Apache half an hour later and filed his complaint. Uncle Sam would probably pay him several hundred dollars for the animal. The way the compensation was calculated, the farmer was paid for the buffalo, the buffalo it would have fathered, and the lost labor of the buffalo and his offspring. We joked that when you saw your federal tax deducted from your paycheck, just remember that it was going to pay for a lot of bull. And based on the taste of the meat in the mess hall on some days, it appeared that quite a few buffalo had been charging at GIs.

I brought the bubblegum machine along on several more village patrols. The kids got a real big kick out of inserting a slug, pushing the lever, and dispensing a tasty gum ball. I brought my camera along a couple of times and shot some great pictures of the kids as they played with the machine. Morale at this time was better than it had been for a while. We got an occasional stand-down, so that helped quite a bit.

My brother Bruce, also in the army, was thinking about going to one of the specialty schools for advanced training. I encouraged him to stay in touch and let me know where he was stationed.

I wrote to Christina and suggested that we start thinking about our future plans after I returned to the States. My plan was to apply for the September MBA program at Michigan State University. We were also discussing a possible wedding date, perhaps in the second half of July. We had some savings and I would have benefits from the GI Bill that would help to get us started.

We had a company stand-down on Saturday, and they brought in several cases of beer. Everyone was feeling pretty good, and a few were feeling no pain by 16:00. Later that evening, I headed to the bridge along with the others in our small group. When we got there we had an unusual opportunity to listen to some good British and American music broadcast from Kuala Lumpur in Malaysia. We were picking it up on a shortwave set belonging to one of the ARVN's at the bridge. It sounded great. We were hoping we would soon see our last night on the bridge. They were bringing in some men from the rear to handle the job.

Things got tense on Sunday night. We heard there was a chance of an attack of some sort, perhaps mortars or a ground attack or both. It was Nixon's first full day in office, and the NLF might launch some type of offensive to test the new president. We also had reports of units of various sizes in the area. It was likely that nothing would happen, but nobody was taking any chances. Everyone was checking weapons, magazines, and grenades. Gas masks and flak jackets were lying on most bunks.

I received a letter from an acquaintance at college mentioning that my friend, Paul, finally received his CO (conscientious objector) classification. Apparently, he got the classification "...but had to take a lot of insults to get it." I chose a different path, but I respected Paul for his beliefs. He had always been consistent in his opposition to the war.

We went out on a sweep on Tuesday, which turned out to be a quiet day. When we returned to the camp, I started getting my travel items and camera ready for my R&R. I intended to turn in my rifle and other gear the next day.

On Wednesday I went into Di An and picked up a couple of shirts and slacks at the PX. I also had my khakis pressed and had my sergeant's stripes sewn on. When I put on the Class A uniform the next morning, it was the first time since last June that I had worn anything other than green jungle fatigues. It was also a first for shoes, since I had been wearing jungle boots the entire time. I was lucky enough to see a movie at the artillery club on the Di An base. Small things, but they meant a lot.

On Friday, January 24, I sent my brother Gary a new set of South Vietnamese Ranger fatigues. They cost me three cartons of Salem cigarettes, which was not a bad deal, since I didn't smoke, and I got them for free in the SP packs we received. He told me later that they fit him perfectly, and he was delighted with his birthday present. I now had my clean clothes and had taken care of some personal obligations, so I was ready for R&R.

# CHAPTER 12

# R&R—A GREAT WEEK "DOWN UNDER"

I got a ride to Camp Alpha in Saigon, a staging area for men flying out on R&R. We were restricted to the camp, which covered roughly a square block, so I really didn't have an opportunity to see Saigon. The camp was a nice change from the boonies. They had hundreds of magazines and newspapers, a large TV room, and a club that served beer and featured a small band from the Philippines. The band wasn't that good, but they played loud.

My R&R trip to Sydney, Australia, started well and ended well. We left on Sunday, January 26, from Tan Son Nhut Air Base and flew on a World Airways Boeing 707 jet. Everyone on the plane was in a great mood. We were dressed in our Class A, short-sleeve khaki uniforms. We made a refueling stop in Darwin, Australia, a moderate-size facility, clean and quiet. There were kangaroo skins and other items for sale in the gift shop. We reboarded the plane and completed the flight. Everyone was thrilled when the plane finally touched down in Sydney. It was summer in Australia, and the weather did not disappoint.

We got on a bus heading to the USO Center in downtown Sydney and listened to a brief orientation talk explaining hotel/motel options, various trips and excursions, and a reminder to meet back there on time on our scheduled departure date. I signed up for a wa-ter-skiing excursion that was set up for Monday. The USO had a va-riety of brochures for typical tourist sites around Sydney. I spotted a table with a banner stating, THE AMERICAN AUSTRALIAN ASSOCIATION, that was staffed by three mature ladies. They explained that they were able to set up dates for dinner or other public events in Sydney with young women who had signed up to accompany American GIs on leave. While they did not expressly say it, it was made clear that these were "nice" girls who expected to be treated with respect. I signed up and was given a name of a girl who would meet me for dinner at a restaurant in the city.

I booked a room in the Woollahara Travelodge on Wallis Street. The first thing I did was call Christina. She sounded terrific, as if I were calling from a phone booth down the street! We talked for awhile as though I'd been gone only a couple of days. I also called my mother. It was great to have long two-way conversations with-out the interruptions of the MARS calls. I got a ticket to see the New Christy Minstrels, a popular American group that was touring in Australia. That night the concert hall was packed, and it was like attending a college hootenanny. It was good to hear a live American group.

The next morning five other GIs and I boarded a minivan for the ride to the water-ski resort, Torren's Water-Ski Gardens, located at Wiseman's Ferry an hour and a half north of Sydney. It was a great day! We all had an opportunity to spend much of the day skiing on a very wide stretch of river. Alternately, we'd ride in the towboat or relax on the beach. There was plenty of beer and food and great-tasting barbecued steaks for lunch. One of the staff members took a series of pictures of me skiing, so I'd have great memories of that day.

I had chosen Sydney for my R&R destination because it was the farthest point away from my home in New York, and there was nothing else around it. I reasoned that I might travel close to other destinations (such as Bangkok, Hong Kong, Singapore, or Tokyo) in the future, because they were close to other countries that I might visit. Sydney also had the advantage of an English-speaking population. It turned out to be a very comfortable place to visit. The facts that they drove on the left side of the road and spoke with an unusual accent were minor issues for me, since I did not rent a car and guessed that my accent was a challenge for them as well.

I spent the next few days walking around Sydney and taking pictures of various parks, buildings, and historical sites. Some local shots were impressive—a butcher's window with a tray full of pig's heads, and a fireman hosing down a car that had crashed and caught fire. My Australian hostess and I had dinner at a couple of different restaurants during the week. One of the best restaurants was located at the top of the tallest building in Sydney, the Australia Square Tower, a fifty-story round building that had fabulous views of the city and the harbor. Once again, lots of great photos.

I was excited to see everything, the Sydney Harbour Bridge, Royal Botanic Gardens, Bondi Beach, Manly Beach, King's Cross, and the Sydney Opera House. I also took a hydrofoil ride to visit the Taronga Park Zoo.

I photographed exquisite flowers at the Royal Botanic Gardens and a magnificent sculpture of a bronze mare and foal that was created in 1891. King's Cross featured a wide assortment of bars and clubs with several large signs advertising "go-go" girls, very much like Times Square in New York.

The most impressive photographic subject in Sydney was the Sydney Opera House, still under construction, with uniquely designed curved shells that formed the various sections of the building. The Opera House was also Australia's biggest in-joke. They'd had trouble with the architect. They'd been building it for years and had poured eighty million dollars into it already. Everyone had strong feelings about the design, and they were not shy about expressing them.

Harbour Bridge photo taken during R&R from an observation tower in downtown Sydney.

The Sydney Opera House, a work in progress.

I met my local hostess at Manly Beach one afternoon for lunch and a refreshing swim. There were plenty of locals as well as tourists enjoying the beach. No sharks were sighted on the day we visited, but sharks were a concern for locals, who avoided the water when they were present. The hydrofoil boat ride to the Taronga Park Zoo was one of the highlights of my visit. It was a passenger ferry with skis mounted on the front of the boat. As it picked up momentum, the bow lifted out of the water, and we moved at a high rate of speed. I was able to get numerous photos of kangaroos, koala bears, and kookaburras, as well as other animals and birds native to Australia. On the ride back to the city, I photographed a large numbers of boats participating in a sailboat race.

All good things come to an end, including my Sydney visit. I returned to the airport Sunday morning, February 2, and waited in the lounge with lots of other American GIs. We were all exhausted, and a few were heavily hungover, since we stayed up late on our last night prior to going back to Vietnam. A few days later, the *New York Times* carried a photo showing exhausted GIs lying back on the seats in the airport waiting area in Sydney. Christina sent me the picture a couple of weeks later, and I was able to verify that it was an authentic scene.

We finally took off and spent some quiet hours resting on the plane before we landed for a refueling stop. We walked around before reboarding for the final leg. As we approached Tan Son Nhut Air Base, I took a couple of photos from the plane. The dragon-shaped outline of the Saigon River as we flew over confirmed we were in Vietnam. We also passed directly over the water plant and Fort Apache and I was back "home" again.

It was a surprisingly good experience returning to the field, seeing friendly faces, and having everyone ask me how R&R was. No patrols that day, so that made the day even better. Things had been quiet while I was gone, and more new men had joined the company, so the combination of those two factors helped to improve morale. But it didn't take long to get back into the regular routine.

I was soon out on patrols again, conducting search and destroy missions as well as night ambush duty. The first few days were fairly normal. We headed out on foot or on trucks, conducted the patrols or visited a village, returned at night, ate, rested, and repeated this again the next day.

My brother Bruce wrote that he was going through training for radio repair at Fort Benning. It was a good skill and might keep him out of the field if he was sent to Vietnam.

The weather was getting increasingly warm. It was the dry season, and it hadn't rained once in the last three months. It would most likely continue to be hot and dry until the end of May.

We were supposed to move to another camp, but the move was postponed. The next camp I'd be assigned to would probably be my last one, because I was getting *short*! Short referred to length of time left in-country, not physical height. I probably weighed a bit less than when I arrived, but my height had not changed. Short was also used as a term of joy.

The next day we went out on patrol, and after the third river, I was soaked from head to foot. I crawled out, and one of the guys yelled to me, "Welcome back to Vietnam."

They have seasons in Vietnam. Rather than the familiar four seasons, winter, spring, etc. they have two: rainy and dry. The rainy season runs from May to November, and the dry season runs from December to April. We were in the dry season, and the most visible evidence was the end of the rice-growing season and the beginning of the harvest. The average temperature was within a fairly tight range most of the year from eighty to eighty-six degrees Fahrenheit.

It often felt cooler in the rainy season, because we were frequently wet, and the winds were stronger.

One of the other platoons in our company blew an ambush at a road crossing at night, and there was a "mad minute" when everyone was firing away on full automatic. The "minute" was closer to ten minutes, but someone finally called out, "Cease fire." They proceeded forward cautiously, searching for wounded VC or blood trails. The only thing they found was a dead water buffalo that hadn't gotten the word about the night curfew.

The following day we went out on another patrol, one of the wettest in a long time. About thirty minutes out, we crossed a river, and it seemed like we stayed in the water for the rest of the day. If we weren't going through a river we were sloshing through rice paddies. I felt pretty good at the end of the day, sitting on a dry bunk in clean dry clothes. I guess it takes a little misery to enjoy the happiness in life.

We went out on another sweep on Saturday, February 8. The 18th Infantry Regiment had ordered all units to increase the number of patrols while anticipating more enemy activity. Our patrol area was relatively dry, and it turned out to be a quiet day with no enemy contact. We did have more excitement at night. We were living in tin buildings set up with double-deck bunks. The walls were sandbagged up to the first bunk, but not to the second. Around 01:30 I awoke to the sound of several automatic bursts. I dove to the floor, grabbed my helmet, flak jacket, and rifle, and I ran outside to the mortar pits. As I got there, the firing stopped. A man or an animal had set off a trip flare along the wire that surrounded our NDP. One of the bunker guards opened up on it, and several men went to check it out but couldn't find anything. So we all went back to sleep. They said the shorter you got, the more nervous you got. I hoped not, but when I returned to my bunk, half the guys were still asleep and hadn't heard a thing.

The next night another platoon went on ambush patrol and did have contact. They had no casualties but killed one VC.

It was a new day and a wet day. We crossed five large rivers and a dozen smaller streams and tributaries. I felt like a sponge. It looked like our patrols in the boonies were increasing.

We set out on another patrol on Monday, February 10, the worst since we were at the water plant. We encountered rivers all day and thick grass and vines seven or eight feet high. I was on flank, so while the main file only crossed six or seven rivers, my partner and I crossed over a dozen. On one river crossing, my buddy lost his helmet and rifle. We dove in and recovered the rifle but not the helmet. We did not have contact that day, but another nearby unit in boats on a river was ambushed by the Viet Cong. A few of our men were wounded, but no one was killed.

Christina asked me to describe the Vietnamese people. The people we encountered were very quiet and restrained, seldom if ever loud or boisterous. If they were not totally frightened, they were very friendly. When we were on the pacification visits, we would walk along the road and visit various families. In situations like those they would invite us into their homes and offer us a chair and food and fruit. They were always eager to share and put up a front of independence, providing us the best their house had to offer.

More often than not, however, we were not on pacification visits. During these missions, we'd search homes with the presumption that there was a VC hiding there with a grenade or rifle. Imagine the following scenario: It's a warm Sunday afternoon, and you and your family are eating dinner. You are in the middle of a conversation over good food, and you happen to glance toward the door. Three combat soldiers in helmets and boots are pointing rifles at you with their fingers on the triggers. Turning toward the kitchen, you see two more soldiers standing there with rifles. You hear four or five more soldiers checking closets, opening drawers, and looking underneath beds. The soldiers bark orders and point to you, demanding, in a foreign language, to see your ID or driver's license. If you glance outside, you see a half dozen more soldiers surrounding your house. This whole action takes about five minutes. You never heard the soldiers coming, they just suddenly appeared. Your reaction to these events would probably be the same as the Vietnamese, outward compliance masking fear and resentment.

The following day, on another long patrol, we experienced a different view of civilian interaction. We passed by a group of Vietnamese civilians who were in the process of harvesting rice. A very young boy, about six years old, came up to me and said, "GI, give me chop-chop." So I reached into my pocket and gave him a couple of pieces of candy. We then set up in a defensive position and broke for chow. This boy started yakking away, telling me how VC were number ten and GIs were number one. He then tried to sell me a coconut and various other items that were growing nearby. He kept this patter up the entire time I was eating my C-rations. He was very friendly and outgoing.

We left that field and continued on our patrol. Later in the afternoon we stopped in another village. There was a small stream about ten feet wide, and five boys were swimming in the water. They were laughing and having a ball. They were all between seven and nine years old. I was carrying the rope that day, so I uncoiled it and threw it to one of the kids. He swam to the other side, and then I pulled him across very fast. We repeated this towrope game several times. Later I told him to tie it to a tree on the other side. He and the other boys began to pull themselves across and drop into the water. This went on for about half an hour before we finally had to move out. It reminded me of some great times I had swimming as a young boy. Some patrols were not all bad, and the people were often friendly. With the exception of these two stops, we spent the rest of the day crawling through mud, rivers, and undergrowth.

Thursday, February 13, was an interesting day. The platoon went out on patrol, but I did not go with them, because I was asked to photograph the distribution of notebooks to the four or five schools in our area. I was not an official photographer, but the company commander wanted some pictures to pass on to battalion since this was one of the high-visibility projects of the pacification program. We left Fort Apache around 10:00 and found that all of the schools had closed for the Tet holidays. Army intelligence must have screwed up again, since a simple check with the provincial leaders would have alerted them about the annual school closures. In any event, we returned to camp, and I was able to take it easy for the rest of the day. I lucked out for once.

There was another military screw-up that night with more serious consequences. One nearby company (not ours) was set up in an ambush position when they saw movement and opened up. The movement turned out to be another company setting up for an ambush. The second company was in the wrong place and did not know it. When the firing stopped three men were wounded. Two were in critical condition, but the third was still able to walk. The wounded men were dusted off, and they merged the two companies into one large ambush position. This event occurred during a period of aggressive activity on our part in anticipation of a Tet offensive in four days.

I had another exciting day while we were out on a sweep looking for VC tunnels. In the middle of the morning, we found a dry well shaft that had been covered up. We checked it out and saw a snake down the shaft which was about forty feet deep. We dropped a grenade down the shaft and jumped back. After the smoke cleared a bit someone fired a magazine into the well. Our suspicions about this well had been raised because the VC often place snakes in tunnels and wells to discourage GIs from entering.

A "tunnel rat" was needed to go down into the shaft to check it out more closely. I usually didn't get asked to do this job because most tunnels had a very low ceiling which meant that the shorter men got selected. Today, it was my turn, so I became the tunnel rat. Someone handed me a .45-caliber pistol and a few grenades. I figured that if the shrapnel didn't kill the snake, the concussion should have.

I tied the rope and sat in the loop while holding on to the long end of the rope. I was then lowered into the well. About halfway down, I started choking on the fine dust. There was about a foot of water in the well. I didn't find any tunnels branching off, so they pulled me back up. My lungs and throat were burning from the dust, which was a combination of fine dirt and gunpowder. I started chewing gum which provided some relief. We finished the patrol and ended the day without any contact.

They showed a movie in the mess hall that evening. The guys in supply were able to borrow a projector and powered it from a gasoline generator. It was a great treat. The movie was *Hurry Sundown*. The plot was depressing, but it was still good to have a diversion. About a third of the way through the movie, we experienced a real-life diversion. A loud explosion shook the building. Everyone grabbed his weapon and ran outside. As it turned out, some ARVNs had accidently set off a claymore mine in a field near our camp. When everything calmed down, we went back and watched the rest of the movie. The incongruity of the movie and the blast had an unnerving effect. It was difficult to relax or let one's guard down too much, because something would pop up to prove that Vietnam was still a dangerous place.

I sent a serious letter home in mid-February with the following message. "For your information, we've been asked to inform you that death announcements are always made in person by an officer or a senior NCO (sergeant). These are followed by a telegram, never by phone. It seems that there are some crackpots running around making phone calls to the families of servicemen. Ignore them."

On Monday, February 17, the first day of Tet, we were out on patrol near a village and saw visible manifestations of the holiday. The kids who were usually wearing plain or patched clothes had changed into freshly pressed, bright new clothes. Most of the stalls in the marketplace were closed. We stopped there to rest for a few minutes. Suddenly shots were going off all over the place. Everyone hit the dirt, but it turned out to be a couple of kids who had lit a string of firecrackers. We calmed our jangled nerves and finished the day without incident.

The next day we found ourselves on a ten-mile patrol through mud and crud and jungle. It was the worst patrol we'd been on in about four months. We had been going out on patrols for eight days straight without a stand-down. Everyone was fatigued. That night we were on a yellow alert with a possibility of being rocketed. With any luck we wouldn't get hit, but everyone was wearing his web gear, helmet, and flak jacket.

We finally had a stand-down on Friday, February 21. I rode on the supply truck to Di An to take care of some publicity pictures for the pacification programs that we had been conducting. While I was at the service club there, I caught an afternoon movie, titled *In the Heat of the Night*, an excellent movie about racism and mutual respect in the American South. I rode the truck back to Fort Apache and made it in time for chow.

The Red Cross frequently sent books to our camp, and I had some time in the evenings to read. I had finished *The Good Earth* and *Venetian Affair* and was starting *Confessions of an Irish Rebel* by Brendan Behan.

It was a bad night on Sunday, February 23. One of the infantry platoons from our company set up an ambush position about a thousand meters from our NDP near the village of Phouc Binh II. At 03:00 they detected seven Viet Cong within fifty meters of their position. Firing erupted on both sides. The RTO (radio-telephone operator) and the platoon leader maneuvered through the hostile rounds while maintaining communication with HQ. The RTO was firing while moving forward and killed one VC. He understood that illumination was needed to identify the enemy's position, so he fired a series of hand flares that lit up the scene. He was hit by enemy fire and died. He would later be awarded a posthumous Silver Star for his actions. Two other US soldiers were also wounded in this firefight, including the lieutenant.

The VC also rocketed Saigon, Long Binh, and Bien Hoa, and mortared a couple of NDPs near us. It appeared as if there would be a strong Tet offensive. Our mortar platoon went out on a patrol the next day, but we had no contact. Saigon had been hit three times: it would be a long night.

On Monday, February 24, we had contact for the first time in a while. It was my first run-in with the North Vietnamese army since arriving in-country. We came on two enemy soldiers in some thick brush near a river. They were killed in a brief firefight. Fortunately, we did not suffer any casualties. It was obvious that the enemy was becoming more aggressive. It was unusual to make contact during the daytime in our area, since the enemy usually moved only at night.

Things continued to run hot and heavy the following day. While it was a quiet day for our company, a different company in our battalion was mortared again, and another company blew an ambush at midnight. The action continued until 08:00 the next morning. They killed or captured twenty-two VC. Only one of their men was wounded. I was becoming more anxious to get out of there.

We had more action again on Wednesday, February 26. I was sound asleep when I heard that now familiar "Crack! Crack! Ping!"

I hit the floor and put my helmet and flak jacket on. There were rounds flying all over the place. I low crawled over to the mortar pit and uncovered the gun. A few minutes later, the rest of the guys got into the pit, and we started firing illumination rounds so that the men in the bunkers could see where to fire. We had one platoon on ambush about five hundred meters from our NDP. They opened up on the VC located between the ambush position and our camp. When that happened, everyone inside the camp got down, because the shots from the ambush site were landing inside the camp. The whole event lasted about an hour. In the morning, we swept through the area and found one dead VC. Luckily, no one in the NDP or ambush position was hurt. However, bullet holes were everywhere. The mess sergeant found a bullet hole that had penetrated the wall and his mosquito net about six inches above his head. We went out on a search and destroy that day but had no further contact.

Fortunately, the next day was quiet without any contact. The company that took over the NDP we had left in November was not as lucky. They had been mortared several nights in a row. One of their platoons got hit only a thousand meters from that NDP. The fighting had continued throughout the day. Three men were killed, and several were wounded. They now had six companies of infantry surrounding the area, and they were pouring in bombs, artillery, air strikes and gunships. We anticipated that this would go on for a long time. There had also been fighting up at Bien Hoa for three days. Eventually, the fighting at our old NDP ended. They killed quite a few VC, but we wound up losing more GIs. There appeared to be no end in sight to this offensive. I had three and a half months left and felt it would be the longest three and a half months of my life. Although the other units had a quiet night, giving us a break for a day or so, we didn't think the offensive was over yet.

No enemy contact reported as Huey pilots prepare to land in the LZ (landing zone).

Soldiers leave the choppers rapidly and move to the perimeter of the field.

We were out on patrol again on Friday, February 28, and Saturday, March 1, with no contact.

On Monday, March 3, I realized that I had exactly one hundred days left in Vietnam. I took some time to draw up a few short-timer calendars. I sent them to Christina and my family and kept one for myself. It featured a cartoon character, Snuffy Smith, with a grid of one hundred boxes. As each day passed, I would fill in one of the squares until the final day when I would be flying home.

I developed a sore on my foot that had become infected, so I stayed in camp for a few days. I had torn the skin when I jumped out of my bunk the night our NDP was in the middle of the firefight. Several days of walking through wet rivers and jungles did not help the recovery process. The medic cleaned it out, and it was healing better.

One of our platoons blew an ambush one klick from our NDP at night. They didn't get any VC, but some rounds landed in a different ambush position a thousand meters from them. One man was wounded in the foot and was dusted off.

We headed out on another patrol in early March through a pretty dry area, so I brought my camera with me. I wanted to get some photos of the Vietnamese rice harvest before it ended. After moving for an hour or so, we came upon dry rice paddies. Since it was harvest season, the farmers sealed off the paddies to prevent water from entering and allowed the ground to dry out. That made it a great deal easier for us to move over solid ground.

We came upon a field where the harvest was underway. It was fairly quiet, so I was able to shoot a roll of slides when we stopped for a short break. Six people were harvesting rice; four were women, and two were young teenage boys about thirteen or fourteen years old. The women wore the typical black pajama-style pants and white blouses with full-length sleeves. Woven conical hats protected their heads from the sun. One woman wore a cloth scarf wrapped around her head. A small earring was visible under the scarf. She had a subdued dignity about her, enhanced by her simple jewelry. The boys were barefoot and wore shorts. One wore a plain cotton shirt and a blue-and-white-checked fedora. The other wore a green fatigue shirt and a fatigue cap that had probably come from the South Vietnamese army or a US soldier. They attached a South Vietnamese flag to a tall pole in the middle of the field. The bright yellow flag with red stripes was intended to notify ARVN and American troops, such as us, that they were civilians.

We scouted the perimeter of the field and then advanced to the farmers. Since they were women and young boys, we did not check their identification but let them continue with the harvest. Rice was a critical crop for the country, and the pacification policy encouraged the support and protection of the farmers, especially if there was no hostile action in the immediate area.

A Vietnamese woman cuts the sheaves of rice with
a small sickle and stacks the bundles.

A boy shakes the rice grains loose into the base of the wooden sled.

The patrol checks the identity papers of an older farmer.

A couple of the members of our platoon had worked on farms in the United States and were used to tractors and other equipment to get the maximum yield from the land. The South Vietnamese farming methods were primitive by our standards. The rice harvest looked like a system that had not changed in several hundred years. Old women, bent at the waist, stood in the field and grasped a bundle of rice stalks with one hand. With the other hand, they cut the bundle at the base of the stalks with a small sickle. They stacked the bundles of stalks in small piles as they gradually worked their way through the field.

A young boy followed behind them, pulling a small wooden sled with two runners on the bottom that were about five feet long. A short wooden box rose about three feet above the runners. The interior of the box had large walls of woven bamboo rising to a height of about seven feet from the base of the box. These walls enclosed the sides and the back of the box. The front of the sled had a thick wooden bar resting at the top of the box.

As the boy moved along the rows, he collected the piles of rice stalks. He beat the stalks against the thick wooden bar at the top of the box. The rice at the top end separated from the stalks and dropped into the box. When all of the rice had been removed, he placed the barren stalks in a separate pile and continued with new stalks until all the rice had been recovered from the stop. He then advanced to the next pile of rice stalks.

I realized that these farmers had been working since sunrise and had harvested about a third of the field. They would continue this process for the rest of the day and would return the next day to move on to one of the other fields ready to yield this food source so critical for Vietnam. The harvest we witnessed that day was repeated in thousands of fields throughout the country. The disruptions of war had had a negative impact on the yields of the rice fields. The country was capable of meeting the needs of its own population as well as exporting large volumes of rice to the world market, but it was constrained by the political and military demands of two different social and economic systems.

Since we did not have any military reason to stay with these farmers, we passed through their fields and continued our patrol deeper into the countryside until we reached our final point at the end of the day. Trucks met us and returned us to our camp.

One afternoon the platoon sergeant invited me to sit down with him for a personal discussion. I was about three months away from leaving Vietnam, so I suspected that I was about to hear the "re-up" talk. I had guessed correctly. He started out by telling me that I'd been doing a good job and that I had an opportunity to receive a promotion from E-5 (sergeant) to a permanent E-6 (staff sergeant) if I made the commitment to reenlist. This would guarantee me a pay raise and increased responsibility.

I explained that I felt I had a good future in civilian life and would like to own my own business someday. He related his personal experience and explained how he had left the army a few years ago and started a business in Kentucky. That did not turn out well due to stiff competition. He warned me that business was a risky proposition. After losing a great deal of money, he closed the business and reenlisted in the army.

He said that the army needed good men and that I could look forward to steady employment, free meals and housing, and plenty of opportunities for advancement. I told him that I was applying to graduate school and wanted to pursue other opportunities. We ended the meeting, and I returned to my post. He had completed his obligation and could report on some military form that I had been given the re-up talk.

# CHAPTER 13

# FORT PAWNEE

On the morning of Friday, March 7, we went out on a sweep for a few hours then returned to Fort Apache and packed up everything prior to leaving the camp. In the afternoon we loaded our gear on trucks and drove back to Di An. The move went pretty smoothly, and everyone settled in. Since we were now based in Di An, we thought we would be flying out in choppers for the next couple of months.

We went out on a patrol again on Sunday, March 9, in trucks instead of helicopters. The day was pretty much without incident. Our machine gunner got a scare while we were crossing a river. He was pushing his gun across on an air mattress when the current caught him and pulled him under. I was already on the other side. I went after him, grabbed him, and pulled him to shore. He had swallowed a little water but was otherwise OK.

Later in the afternoon we discovered a bunker and a fifteen-foot-tall observation tower hidden in the jungle growth along the river. We blew up the bunker and the tower and then headed back to our pickup point and boarded trucks. Two armored personnel carriers escorted us, providing security on the open road. Ironically, as we moved along, one APC broke down. Then, 500 meters farther down the road, the other one broke down. So much for security...we did make it back safely.

My responsibilities as sergeant still included FO; however, the artillery FO, a lieutenant, had been going out with the ambushes, so it was not necessary for me to go along. Instead, I went on patrols with my platoon doing various jobs such as carrying a radio, rope, etc., in addition to my M-16.

Morale was pretty good, probably because we were kept pretty busy. The flip side was that we hadn't had a stand-down in a long time, and everyone was becoming exhausted again. Otherwise, I was doing OK.

"SHORT!" As of Tuesday, March 11, I had exactly three months left in Vietnam. This was a significant milestone. We started out the day with an uneventful sweep, i.e., no contact and no booby traps. At the end of the afternoon, however, we did get a surprise from command. Instead of going back to Di An as planned, they dropped us off at an NDP in the boonies called Fort Pawnee. We were supposed to be there temporarily—for two or three days—to secure the place while the resident company was somewhere else on a special operation. All we had with us were our razors, our toothbrushes, and our weapons.

The days started to stretch out as we continued to live at this "temporary" NDP. It now appeared that we would be at Fort Pawnee for a week or more. Most of our personal gear was back at Di An, and we had just the bare necessities.

Thursday was a particularly hectic day. We were out on patrol all day in the mud and crud. At the end of the day, we found an old VC tunnel that looked like it had been abandoned. The vegetation around the entrance was checked for booby traps and then cleared away. We then lay on the ground as someone threw a grenade into the tunnel. One of the smaller guys was assigned to be the tunnel rat. He removed his pack, waited a few minutes for the dust to clear, then started crawling into the three-foot-high tunnel with a .45-caliber pistol. It was a short tunnel, only ten or fifteen feet into the ground.

The tunnel rat crawled back out and reported his observations. There were some old wooden boxes and a couple of glass bottles, but he saw no evidence that anyone had been in the tunnel for a long time.

The lieutenant reported the location and contents of the tunnel to battalion headquarters. They sent word back to blow it up and continue with the mission. One of the other soldiers wrapped up some C-4 in a small bundle, placed it in the tunnel, and ran a wire from the bundle to a point about fifty feet away. We all hit the dirt as he yelled, "Fire in the hole" and detonated the explosive. The tunnel entrance collapsed as a column of dust and smoke rose from the spot. The tunnels that we found in our area tended to be much smaller and shorter in length than those found elsewhere in Vietnam. That is why we blew up the entrance after a quick inspection. The tunnels at Cu Chi, which was only twenty miles from Saigon, were very long and sophisticated and included sleeping quarters, hospitals and supply rooms for the Viet Cong and NVA troops.

We resumed our patrol and then headed back to camp. We received more reports of enemy movement in our area. Everybody in the camp at Fort Pawnee was on heightened alert. The number of men on guard duty was doubled. For a while it had seemed that things were getting better, but suddenly events seemed to be deteriorating. We were not having as much contact as we were when we were flying out of Di An, but things were still pretty tense.

About this time, there was a renewed emphasis on pacification in our area. We received the usual orders to visit a village and try to build goodwill with children and adults. The platoon boarded trucks, and we headed out on our mission with several cartons of small notebooks. The outside and inside covers featured a short comic-book version of *Batman and Robin* in Vietnamese that described a story of the masked duo capturing some evil person. The rest of the notebook was filled with blank pages to be used to record lessons.

Fort Pawnee, our "temporary" base, where we stayed longer than we expected.

The village "smithy" converts an aluminum flare casing into a metal pot.

When we arrived at the location, we looked for any unusual signs of activity and proceeded to set up a perimeter around the village. Some of the platoon headed for the primary school that had several classrooms. The teachers, all women, had been notified in advance that we would be coming with books for the children. The children were separated—boys on one side of the classroom and girls on the other. The lieutenant, platoon sergeant, and our interpreter entered each class and spoke with the teacher.

A couple of our guys started to pass out the books to the children. This change in their routine unleashed a buzz of excitement in the room, and the teacher calmly reminded the children to quiet down.

I noticed some interesting contrasts in the scene. Our burly, gruff platoon sergeant with the thick mustache knelt next to the desk of a young boy and handed him one of the books. The young boy thanked him for the book in Vietnamese, and they briefly smiled at each other. The other incongruity was the sight of rifles hanging from the shoulders of each soldier as we moved from class to class.

When most of the books had been distributed, we stepped into the courtyard of the school for a few minutes before leaving. The platoon sergeant stopped to speak with a Vietnamese Catholic nun who was in charge of an orphanage next to the school. He handed her the remainder of the notebooks. She flashed a big bright smile and thanked him for the gift.

As we moved through the village heading to our pickup point, we passed a small shop where a tinsmith was working with aluminum and other metal items. He had a mixed collection of US military items and other metal debris that had obviously been gathered from the sites of recent skirmishes. There were pieces from large shell casings, large and small flares, and other items. His primary source of income appeared to be from the sale of metal pots. He displayed several pots of various sizes ranging from one quart to five gallons.

He was working on a large pot, pounding the aluminum into shape with a ball peen hammer. We clearly saw the words stamped on the piece of aluminum, "US Navy, Flare, Aircraft." It was good to see some of our expended ordnance being put to good use, but we also wondered if pots and pans were his only business. We realized his metalworking skills could also be used to produce enemy weapons such as mines and booby traps. He also could be in the business of repairing weapons for Viet Cong forces in the area, but this was supposed to be a friendly village, and we were on a pacification mission, so we ignored the shop and moved on to the pickup area.

Our old platoon sergeant, Moore, went home and was replaced by a new lieutenant from Texas, who was running the platoon. The new guy was OK. I was now the acting platoon sergeant and the middleman between the platoon leader and the squad leaders. I still went out in the field but was also responsible for handling sick calls, supplies, and other things guaranteed to keep me busy.

We were supposed to get a senior NCO to take over as platoon sergeant, but he never showed up, so I remained the acting platoon sergeant for several more days and dealt with the expected headaches that came with the job.

On Monday, March 17, I sent a letter to Christina, who is Irish, and wished her a happy Saint Patrick's Day. "In honor of Saint Patrick's Day today, the entire company wore green pants and green shirts." In her next letter she acknowledged the marginal humor.

That night it poured for three hours, the first rain in a long time. We continued on heightened alert, because enemy activities had continued to escalate. We officially took over Fort Pawnee on March 18, when the few people remaining from the other unit left. We went back to Di An to bring out the rest of our gear and our mortars. It looked as if we'd be there for quite a while.

Sergeant Jones, a senior NCO, finally arrived on the night of March 18 and took over on a permanent basis, so I was relieved of the extra duties. I hoped to be able to write more letters and take some pictures. We continued our sweeps every day. We felt some sense of stability, since we now knew that we would be at Fort Pawnee for some time.

Later that week we boarded trucks, left the fort, and headed down the road on a new patrol. As we drove along the road, we passed a convoy of South Vietnamese troops heading in the opposite direction. They had tanks at the front and the rear manned by ARVN troops and about eight trucks and jeeps filled with more ARVNs. It appeared that they were heading off to some objective farther north. There was some resentment within our company because our only contact with ARVN soldiers was when we passed them as they guarded bridges and villages while we proceeded into the boonies for ambushes or search and destroy missions. It was widely felt that we did more fighting, and they did more guarding. The share of risk seemed unfair. That day we saw a group that looked like they were actually going somewhere to fight.

We continued with our sweep and finished early. It had been a short mission that day, so we thought we'd have a stand-down for the rest of the day when we returned to camp.

Our good mood was short-lived. When we return to Fort Pawnee, we found out that we would be moving back to Di An the following day. For the third time in two weeks, we packed up our gear and our mortars and moved the entire company. I tried to be reasonably optimistic and make the best of each day, but it was becoming increasingly hard. I was exhausted and getting worn out with the constant uncertainty.

I opened the package with the birthday cake Christina sent me. I wanted to save it for my birthday in three days, but since we had to move, I shared it with a couple of buddies and then started packing.

The next morning, moving day, we loaded our gear on trucks that headed to Di An. In the meantime, we flew out on choppers to an area where five VC had been sighted. Since we found no one, they picked us up and flew us to another location where two VC had been sighted and one had been wounded. Again, we found no one, so we finally headed back to Di An to sort out our gear. Another search and destroy was scheduled for the next day.

We awoke to some good news! The search and destroy was canceled, and we got a well-deserved stand-down instead. But even after a day of taking it easy, we were still exhausted. Ambush patrols were planned for the coming days, and I was not looking forward to them, but I convinced myself that if I could get through the next few weeks, it would be OK.

March 23 was my birthday. At about 16:00 that afternoon the choppers picked us up and flew us to a new position. The wind was extremely gusty, and it was one of the roughest rides of my entire tour. I thought that the ship would flip over a couple of times, and I was getting airsick. They dropped us off in the middle of a miserable field. The ground was wet, and the tide would be coming up in another few hours. We'd be there all night, set up in an ambush position. I was not having much luck with holidays that year. As a matter of fact, things seem to be worse on a holiday.

I broke eighty days on March 24! Just seventy-nine days left in Vietnam. I was hoping I'd make it. I wrote a letter to Christina in the fading daylight with the grease pencil that I normally used on my map.

The next day we flew back to Di An, and I had some time to pack up a couple thousand black-and-white negatives and a few hundred black-and-white prints and mail them home. They were an important record of my time in Vietnam, and I wanted to be able to review them at some point in the future when I had the time to evaluate the people and events and their meaning during this period of my life.

The chopper flights to the ambush sights started earlier every afternoon. At 16:00 we'd be sitting in a wood line at the edge of a river. We'd stay there until dark and then move into our ambush site.

It turned out to be a hazardous twenty-four hours. While we were getting off the trucks prior to boarding the choppers that afternoon, a rifle went off. One of the guys shot himself in the foot. He claimed that it was an accident, but nobody believed him. Most likely he would be court-martialed. He was scheduled to leave four days before me and was getting scared because he was getting short.

In the morning while we were waiting to be picked up and flown back to camp, we heard an explosion a thousand meters away. Another platoon at a different ambush site found a sampan in the river in the morning. One of the guys threw a grenade to destroy it, but the grenade got caught in a tree. He was injured with shrapnel wounds in his chest, and he was dusted off. He was in fair condition.

I wasn't scared yet, but I was starting to wish that I could get out of the field. A few more weeks on ambush, and I could see myself becoming more nervous. The days were going along pretty fast, but not fast enough. I was also impatiently waiting to see my fiancée in June.

On Wednesday, March 26, I wrote a letter to Christina while in the field. "We are reporting today from deep inside a wet, muddy rice paddy dike as we prepare to set up our night ambush. Yesterday turned out to be rather uneventful, especially considering the previous night. The most exciting thing that happened was at midnight when I went from seventy-eight to seventy-seven days left in-country. I received my application for Michigan State about a week and a half ago, and at that time I wrote to Manhattan College requesting a transcript that I needed. I was really surprised when I got the mail at camp today to see the transcript waiting there, since I didn't expect it that fast. I'll get a money order on payday, and I should have the application in the mail on April 2."

Thursday, March 27, was another hazardous night. Before dark we were directed to set up our ambush on a rice paddy dike in the middle of an open field eight hundred meters wide. The strategy was whichever side you were fired on, you could just jump to the other side of the dike and have protection from incoming rounds. People from a nearby village watched the entire time. About an hour after dark, rounds started coming in just above our heads and into the dike itself. We jumped to the other side of the dike and called in the contact. Due to obvious poor planning and no communication—or something more sinister—the rounds were coming from an ARVN compound nearby. Frequently, those guys just fired their rifles to hear them go bang. The firing stopped, but while we were on the side of the dike, somebody spotted movement at the edge of the field. It was nothing, but if it had been VC, we would have been caught in a cross fire. We were placed in harm's way. We literally and actually dodged a bullet and avoided a potential tragedy. It was the worst night in a long time.

The chaos continued on Friday, March 28. The VC shot down a helicopter in the morning, five hundred meters from the ambush site that we had just left. Our battalion commander was killed, and the deputy commander was wounded. Later that day, they shot down two helicopter gunships, a pretty bold feat, because the last thing that a VC wanted to do was attract the attention of a gunship. By midafternoon a total of four VC had been sighted, and ten had been killed. Our ambush site was an exit route from the area of contact, and everyone was a bit nervous, carrying extra magazines and grenades. Fortunately, we had a quiet night.

We were very busy preparing ambush sites, and there was no time for sleeping most days, let alone writing letters. On Saturday, we got into position in the late afternoon. The other half of our platoon was setting up for an ambush two thousand meters from us. While they were setting up, they disturbed a bee's nest in a tree, and one man had to be dusted off with severe stings about the face and head. Then about 23:00 they blew the ambush on one VC, who managed to get away. Unfortunately, the VC succeeded in shooting our platoon sergeant in the leg before escaping. The medevac chopper returned so that he could be dusted off. I was again the acting platoon sergeant.

# CHAPTER 14

# RIVER PATROL BOATS—CAT LAI

On Sunday, March 30, our platoon experienced a welcome change of scenery. In the late afternoon, we were trucked to Cat Lai, a seaport located at a position near Saigon on the Dong Nai River where it was half a mile wide. This was where they brought in most of the ammunition for Vietnam. A large gray navy cargo ship was anchored in the middle of the river, and two large tugboats were passing the cargo ship on our side of the river.

There was a large structure built on a deck over the water. A sign read "Cat Lai Logistics Command Office, US Army Terminal." Next to the terminal office was a wooden pier. There were two rows of five river patrol boats (PBRs) flying South Vietnamese flags lined up next to the dock in a "raft up" manner, with the first boat tied to the dock lengthwise, and the next four boats tied side to side to the first boat. These boats had been provided by the United States but were maintained and operated by the South Vietnamese navy.

Their fiberglass hulls were painted the standard olive drab. They were thirty-one feet long and armed for battle with a twin .50-caliber machine gun in the front (in a rotating tub), and a .50-caliber machine gun mounted on the back. There was also a distinctive three-foot-diameter radar dome that sat above the cabin.

We took off our gear and sat on the dock, while the Vietnamese crews loaded ammo on their boats and filled the fuel tanks. We were told we'd be going out on a night ambush mission, so we waited for the sun to get lower in the sky.

We finally boarded the PBRs and moved out at high speed (maximum speed twenty-eight knots), churning the water behind us, leaving a wake along the river. As our drop-off point came into view, the boats slowed down and moved closer to the shoreline. We had gone about ten miles along the river, and it was almost dark as we reached our destination. The boats moved toward the edge of the river, gliding to a stop in the mud along the shore. We got off the boats and moved forward through the marshy vegetation. We tried to find some drier spots along the berm before settling in for the night. We set up the standard L-shaped ambush then took turns on watch and tried to get some sleep as the night wore on. There was no contact that night.

PBRs (river patrol boats) take us to a night ambush
site on the Dong Nai River late in the day.

Some time to reflect while the boats move along the river.

We prepared to leave the ambush site at 03:00, earlier than usual but necessary, since the ebb tide would be too shallow at daybreak. The pickup was surreal, almost beautiful, much like a movie. As the boats returned and slowly passed by, we blinked a strobe light for five seconds. They cut their engines and coasted into shore. We blinked a flashlight once, and they blinked back. They pushed up to the shore, and we silently boarded. The timing was exquisite! It was a beautiful moonlit night, and we were speeding down a moonlit river about a half mile wide in boats similar to the PT boats from World War II. It was a remarkable experience. When we returned to Cat Lai, trucks were waiting to return us to camp. Fortunately, I had my camera with me and was able to capture quite a few pictures.

Tuesday, April 1, was a pretty serious April Fools' Day. We were picked up from an ambush site at 08:30, and then we went out again at 14:30. Trucks dropped us off on a quiet road. We headed into some open fields and then moved toward a village. When we reached it, we surrounded it and then carefully walked through. We knew it to be a friendly village, so we took some time to talk with the people and show them that we were allies. Like most villages we visited, it was populated by women, children, and old men.

We saw children resting in hammocks and old women and young girls carrying babies on their hips. The biggest excitement of the day occurred in a backyard, where two roosters were screeching and clawing each other. This fight went on for twenty minutes before the smaller rooster had had enough and walked away.

In the backyard of another home was a large stack of firewood. The woodpile looked like it belonged in New England rather than a small village in the flat delta of South Vietnam. They used the wood for cooking, since it was a cheap source of fuel. The woodpile did look out of place on such a hot day. It never got very cold in this area, and even the Vietnamese winters were relatively mild.

Eventually, we left the village and followed a flat dirt trail lined with small bamboo trees on the left side. It was an easy walk on the hard and flat trail, but we knew it was dangerous. The platoon leader ordered everyone to walk on the left and right of the trail and to be on the lookout for mines or booby traps. Piles of dried leaves next to the trail could easily conceal trip wires tied to grenades or other explosive devices.

We came to a cemetery surrounded by a wire fence. The point man checked the fence for trip wires and found none. Finding a weak spot, he pulled the fence wire off the ground and slid underneath. Everyone in the file followed him. We walked through the rows of graves marked by flat white stone monuments topped with crosses. It appeared to be a relatively new cemetery, probably Catholic, since there was a Catholic school nearby.

We left the cemetery and followed a single set of railroad tracks that led back to our pickup point. Using caution, we stayed some distance from the tracks and the trail and moved off to the right, working our way through the moderate growth of shrubs and trees that paralleled the tracks. We welcomed the hard, dry and dusty ground after months of slogging through wet mud. We finally reached our pickup point. The unending pace of our patrols was getting worse. The whole platoon needed some rest. The rumor was that we were supposed to get a stand-down in five or six days.

A bit of good news. My fabulous new Nikon F camera arrived. I wouldn't dare bring it out to the boonies on patrol, so I repacked it and mailed it home.

The next night I was sitting in the boonies waiting for dark writing a letter. A helicopter flew near us and started firing over our heads at a sampan in the river about 150 meters from us. We hadn't heard the helicopter coming and thought it was VC firing. Some guys were frantically digging into the mud. It was a frightening experience.

Wednesday was another action-packed day. The choppers picked us up in the morning and took us back to Di An. As soon as we landed, the first sergeant told us to eat fast and get our gear ready, because we were moving back to Fort Apache for three days. Fort Apache was the NDP where we were located from November through March during pacification. Following orders, I ate fast and raced to the barracks to complete my graduate school application for Michigan State. I dropped it in the mailbox, grabbed my essential gear, and made it to the truck just as it headed out to the "camp du jour."

We were now back at Fort Apache and living with temporary gear again. We still went out on ambushes, as army life continued its own rhythms. On the bright side, I broke seventy days that afternoon. SHORT!

When I realized that I would be home in a little more than two months, I was anxious to confirm a wedding date in July with

Christina. Mail was sluggish, but I wrote and suggested either spending a week or two honeymooning on some Caribbean island or spending five or six weeks on an extended camping adventure through New England.

I figured that the cost of the two options might be roughly equal, but option two would allow us more time together without work or family responsibilities that were certain in the years to come. Camping would be easy for me. I was used to sleeping outdoors and satisfied with the basic necessities of food and shelter in the warm summer months.

Christina had some experience living in primitive conditions, having spent three summers during college working on a volunteer project in remote Mexican villages. She and her project mates had some interesting adventures of their own, making the best of tough situations.

Ironically, I received a letter from Christina describing work and news of our friends. The letter ended with a PS asking if we were still planning to get married. I realized that our letters had crossed in the mail. I immediately sent a response saying yes and mentioned that she would probably have received my honeymoon suggestions by then. I also got specific on the timeframe: the second or third week of July. In an age before e-mail, communication was painfully slow.

One morning in early April, we ate a quick breakfast and boarded trucks for another day-long patrol. We passed near a village before heading out into more remote areas. It had not rained for some time, so the ground was topped with a powdery layer of white dust. As infantry soldiers, so much of our time was spent walking that we became familiar with the color, texture, and moisture of the ground. We studied it for dangerous objects like wires, piles of dead leaves, or other indications of hostile intent. We watched for small depressions or ditches that might provide temporary safety in the event of a sudden attack.

That morning's route took us through slightly elevated areas covered with small trees, grass, and bushes instead of the familiar palm trees and rice paddies. Eventually, we came to a narrow road that led to the entrance of a compound. A large wooden gate was set inside an imposing square cement arch, surrounded by a thin forest of tall trees. The arch was painted white and at the top was a large wooden-spoked wheel, similar to a ship's steering wheel. Below the wheel were two flags: a South Vietnamese flag on the right and a Buddhist flag on the left. We had seen the colorful Buddhist flag before in various shrines located in the homes of villages we had visited. It had five vertical stripes of blue, yellow, red, white, and orange next to a set of shorter horizontal stripes in the same colors.

On either side of the arch were two small statues of squatting lions. We were struck by the words painted in Vietnamese across the top of the arch and along the side columns. "Buu Quang Tu" (Buu Quang Pagoda Temple), "Buông Thể Mít Mu Tâm Màn Bây Tôi. Của Thiên Thành Tình Muốn Kiếp Nên Duyên" (We are all in a state of confusion, clueless...Deep down, we all want to connect, to build a relationship with our Almighty, who waits for us at the Heavenly Gate).

We passed through the open gate and into the compound. We had standing orders to respect religious buildings and dwellings, but they were not off-limits for inspection to confirm they were not harboring Viet Cong soldiers or weapons. There were several small structures spread out inside the compound. One was a single-story building open on three sides, containing an altar with two painted statues of Buddha in red robes. The rear statue was a sitting Buddha with a large gold halo. Just in front of this was a reclining Buddha.

To the left of the statues was a black-and-white photograph of a Buddhist monk with his eyes closed.

We didn't recognize the monk in the photo, but it may have been the Buddhist monk who set himself on fire in Saigon in 1963. He was protesting the policies of the South Vietnamese government lead by President Ngo Dinh Diem at the time. Diem had been accused of favoring the Catholic minority and repressing Buddhists in appointments to civilian and military offices. He was assassinated later in the year as a result of a military coup and his perceived repressive policies. At the time, more than 80 percent of the country was Buddhist, with Roman Catholics making up most of the remainder of the population.

As we continued through the compound, we were impressed by the neat and orderly layout. Except for one or two monks who remained in their dwellings, it appeared deserted. We guessed the monks were working in nearby fields or visiting villages. The first residence was a two-story stucco structure, roughly fifteen feet wide and twenty feet long, on a square cement pad. It was a simple design with a large open window on each side on both the lower and upper levels. The roof was cone shaped and covered with ceramic tiles. A unique feature of the building was a balcony extending out from the second floor so the occupant could walk around all sides of the building and observe the rest of the compound. Perhaps this was the home of the "head monk."

Farther down the main path was a row of individual structures, resembling a line of miniature homes in a US suburb. Each structure was built in the center of a minilot roughly fifty feet square. In the center of the lot was a cement pad with four large posts supporting a single room on the second floor. The construction was similar to the first building, with stucco walls, a peaked ceramic roof, and a window on each side. The occupant climbed to the room above using a ladder built on one side. There was a door on the side with the ladder leading to a small porch on that side of the building.

A structure in the Buddhist compound.

Finally, we came upon a stone well atop a cement pad in the center of the compound, most likely the water source for cooking and cleaning. We also noticed several well-tended banana trees spread around the area, full of hundreds of bananas in large bunches nearly ready to harvest.

The layout, design, and construction of the buildings, and the well and the gardens, reflected an organized life and an excellent understanding of architecture, engineering, and agriculture. The contrast between the monks' peaceful, methodical life here and the tortuous conflict going on in the rest of the country was striking. It seemed that these Buddhist monks represented a faith and belief system that provided a steady compass to guide the South Vietnamese people through this difficult time.

We spread out and paused to eat lunch. We had been there for perhaps an hour, but it felt like we had attended a religious retreat with a bit of time to contemplate a different approach to life. When our C-rations were consumed, we picked up our gear, moved out of the compound, and continued the patrol. The peacefulness of that day remained with me for a long time.

The next day we were trucked to a drop-off point and started moving through a relatively dry area on another search and destroy mission. The day progressed quietly, with no enemy contact. We broke for a quick lunch and continued moving through a small village and then into some dry, open fields. The point man spotted an opening in the ground, and we stopped to check it out. It was another tunnel.

A new man stepped forward for tunnel rat duty. This tunnel had a bigger opening, about five feet in diameter, so he would have no trouble as he moved through on his hands and knees. We checked the entrance for trip wires or booby traps. There were none. We all hit the ground as another soldier threw a grenade into the tunnel. We waited a few minutes, and when we didn't hear any sounds from the tunnel, the volunteer removed his gear, took a flashlight, several grenades, and a .45-caliber gun from the lieutenant, and headed into the tunnel. The tunnel was dark and filled with the acrid smell of gunpowder and damp earth. It was hard to see or breathe, because there was still a great deal of dust and smoke in the air.

We all understood that he was tense and nervous. Checking tunnels was one of the most dangerous assignments for a soldier. While waiting in an ambush at night or walking with a patrol through open fields, there was obvious danger, but he knew that he had comrades to his left and right, and he was just a small part of a general target. Here, he was a single, specific target hemmed in by dirt walls on all sides. There were too many unknowns in the tunnel. He didn't know its length. He didn't know if there was a single enemy soldier or a dozen. We made a great deal of noise when we discovered the tunnel, and the noise of the grenade would definitely have warned anyone of our presence, even if they were sleeping a long distance back. If it was a long tunnel with other tunnels branching off, there would be plenty of places for Viet Cong to hide and then fire at him as he crawled through the entrance.

He was not happy with this assignment, but he knew that others had taken their chances in other tunnels, and the risk needed to be spread around. If he could get through this tunnel safely, he would not have to do this again for several weeks or months. Determined to get through it, he moved slowly forward with the cocked .45 in his right hand and the flashlight in his left hand.

As he moved forward he shone the light up and down, then left and right. The tunnel was simply a horizontal hole in the dirt. He might be concerned that the grenade blast weakened the ceiling and walls of the cave. There were no reinforcing timbers to hold up the roof. He tried not to consider the consequences of being buried alive. He knew our patrol was carrying a couple of entrenching tools, but it would take some time to dig through if the tunnel collapsed behind him. He focused on the immediate objective. Shine the flashlight, move forward, keep his finger on the trigger. As he crawled forward, he started to see a wall of dirt in front of him. Then he saw the opening ahead veer to the right. He moved forward a couple more feet and shone the light to the right. Once again he saw a wall of dirt to the right. There were no other openings. He had reached the end of a short tunnel, only twenty feet in length. There was no evidence of anyone having been in there for a long time. He had been in the tunnel for less than five minutes, but it seemed like hours. He crawled back out and was happy to breathe clean, fresh air. He stood up and smiled, then provided a brief report. The task was over.

The tunnel location was called in to battalion. We were given instructions to blow it up and then continue with our patrol. A large block of C-4 plastic explosive was wrapped around the end of a long branch, and a blasting cap was placed in the C-4. A wire was also attached to the explosive, and the end of the branch was placed at the tunnel entrance. We all moved back, and the C-4 was detonated. A tall black cloud of smoke and dust rose about seventy-five feet above the ground. We waited a few minutes then went back to check the entrance, now a pile of dirt requiring some time to dig out if someone wanted to reopen the cave. We gathered our gear, continued moving along the tree line at the edge of the fields, and returned to camp.

We had found more tunnels in the last few weeks than in my first eight months in the field, partially due to the dry weather and the drying of the foliage protecting the entrances. Also, our patrols took us into different areas at slightly higher elevations, where the tunnels were more functional for the enemy. Tunnels dug into the berms surrounding rice paddies were likely to fill with water, while the higher terrain allowed them to stay drier and more useable.

On Monday, April 7, we finally got a stand-down, and a group of us headed by truck to the Di An USO. The USO was housed in a large white building, surrounded by sandbag walls and barbed wire. It was located in the village of Di An, about a mile and a half from the US base camp of Di An. I saw a movie (*Anzio,* a war movie), had a milk shake and a couple of hot dogs, and played the piano for a while. Simple stuff, but it was a relief to relax for a couple of hours.

On Tuesday, we headed out for another daytime sweep. On the side of the road where the trucks dropped us off, there was an old man with large metal boxes built around his bicycle containing various food items, including loaves of French bread. Most of the village markets that we passed through had at least one vendor selling these long golden-brown loaves. Rice was the principal starch in the diet throughout Asia and Southeast Asia, and most of the people we encountered at mealtime were eating rice and vegetables, but others were enjoying French bread. The long history as a French colony had apparently left a culinary mark on the country. The French had been gone since the fifties, but their bread remained.

We passed through a dry rice paddy, where several villagers were finishing their rice harvest. It was a small group, two women and a man who appeared to be in his fifties. As we had seen in other villages, they were using the same sickles and wooden sleds to haul the rice.

Ahead of us we saw a small cluster of abandoned houses built on cement pads with stucco walls. There was evidence of earlier battles. Many of the walls were missing or partially demolished. Bullet holes were visible in most of the structures. We walked carefully through the area and looked for any signs of Vietcong activity, then surrounded the area. After confirming that a secure perimeter had been set up, we broke for lunch. We had already walked a long distance that day and crossed several small rivers. Everyone was wet, hot, and tired. After eating our C-rations, we tried to grab a quick nap before leaving. Heading out of the village, we came to a wire fence supported by wooden posts. There was a trail on the other side. The point man knelt near the base of the fence and held a small mirror at arm's length as he checked to see if anyone was on the trail. No one was visible, so we crossed under the wire and moved along the trail. The afternoon passed uneventfully, and we returned to Fort Apache.

We experienced a pleasant change of pace on Wednesday when we stopped at an ARVN compound near a river inlet that we had visited in late November. We set up our own security and took turns swimming for about two hours in the hot sun. It was the first time we'd been swimming recreationally since our last visit. Half a dozen GIs were diving off a partially sunk barge into the water that was extra deep because of a high tide. Several young boys from the village jumped into the river to join in the fun. They showed off their diving skills from the top of the cabin of the barge and challenged us to do the same. Some guys did a passable job at diving, while most executed awkward-looking belly flops.

One of the other sergeants, who wasn't a good swimmer, was reluctant to join us. Finally, he ripped off his shirt, climbed to the top of the barge, and dove in. The exhilaration was contagious, and several others jumped in. After an hour in the water, we crawled out of the river and put our gear back on, giving the half of the platoon that was maintaining security a chance to swim. We also spent some time interacting with the ARVN soldiers and their families, which was part of the reason for stopping there. The swimming session was a big morale booster for everyone in the platoon. When it was time to leave the village, we headed back to our base.

Each time we came through the base gate, everyone removed the magazine from his weapon and held the chamber cover open to show that there were no rounds in the chamber. The purpose of this procedure was to reduce the chance of a weapon accidentally discharging while in the base camp. We lived and slept with our rifles nearby. If we were attacked, we could jam a magazine into the bottom of the rifle very quickly and be ready for anything.

We heard some bad news on Thursday, April 10. Things were going smoothly on the patrol until I heard a report over the battalion radio that the NDP where we were stationed from September to November had just been mortared, and twenty-five rounds landed inside the wire. They returned fire and managed to hold the base. Several men were dusted off. This event raised my anxiety level, and once again I wished I was out of the field. I continued counting the days.

Saturday was a better day; I broke sixty days. Fifty-nine left. The lieutenant injured his foot and had not gone out for two days. As the acting platoon sergeant, I had to take the platoon out both days. I was fortunate and brought everyone back alive. The following day we were supposed to have a stand-down, and I was hoping to get into Saigon to take some pictures.

Members of the patrol board trucks and APCs (armored personnel carriers) for the ride back to camp.

Memorial statue in Saigon.

A group of women wearing the traditional ao dai in downtown Saigon.

On Sunday, April 13, I did get the opportunity to visit Saigon. At 07:30 another sergeant and I hitched a ride in a jeep with a soldier who was on his way to Tan Son Nhut Air Base. We arrived at the air base, had breakfast, then went to a movie while waiting for the PX to open at noon. After picking up several rolls of film, we took a cab to downtown Saigon and spent the next few hours seeing the sights and taking pictures.

Saigon was a big beautiful city. Life seemed so normal; you would never suspect there was a war going on. We stopped at the Saigon USO, had some hot dogs and milk shakes, and relaxed for a while. There was a seamstress there who made the ao dai, the Vietnamese national costume. I wanted to order one for Christina. It had to be specifically fitted, so the woman provided a list of measurements that I later mailed to her along with recommendations on color choices—dark pants and a light dress or light pants and a dark dress. At the end of the day we took a cab back to our NDP.

A couple of weeks after my trip to Saigon, Christina mailed back the measurements. She also asked why I was carrying a rifle in some of the Saigon pictures I had sent her. I explained that there were frequent bombings of GIs in Saigon, especially at bus stops and other places where they congregated. We were not allowed outside our NDP without a weapon and a helmet.

We had a quiet patrol on Monday, but Tuesday was a different story. We were out with another platoon in some extremely muddy, thick vegetation. It was the hottest day in six months. One man was dusted off for heat exhaustion in the middle of the day. Later in the afternoon we encountered two VC, and a brief firefight ensued. They were clearly outnumbered. One was killed, and the other taken prisoner. No one in either platoon was injured. We ran low on water due to the heat and the activity, so they had a helicopter fly in ten gallons of water. It was an exhausting day, and everyone was worn out.

We had a stand-down on Wednesday so I was able to ride the supply truck to Di An and made a MARS call to Christina. There was no answer, so I called my family. It was good talking with them. They expressed concern for my safety and were eager for my return. I let them know that I was just as anxious to get back home. They mentioned that they had been receiving the letters, pictures, and negatives that I had been sending them. My brother asked how I got the black-and-white pictures printed. The film was processed at a place called Coupon Photo in Alabama. They'd process the film and then send me a new roll of film. It was easier dealing directly with the processor. It usually took about two weeks for the printed pictures to get back to me. This method had two advantages over the PX. I was not able to get to the PX in Di An very often, and the processing was done by Vietnamese contractors; the quality was inferior. Many of the black-and-white photos that I took in the early months of my tour had dirt on the negatives, and the prints were often under- or overexposed.

On Thursday and Friday, we participated in a simple pacification project. We brought several cases of vegetable oil packed in one-gallon cans to distribute in a nearby village. The local residents lined up with a variety of glass bottles and jars, and several of our guys transferred the oil into their containers. The cooking oil was an expensive commodity, and the villagers seemed very appreciative. We also passed out some more of the Vietnamese *Batman* notebooks to the children in the village.

While we were in the village, one of our soldiers decided to give his M-16 a quick cleaning. He set the weapon down on the tile porch of a small home. A few of us stayed nearby in case a problem developed. As soon as he separated the stock from the barrel, four young boys started talking excitedly in Vietnamese. Through a combination of finger-pointing and sign language, they indicated that they wanted to disassemble and reassemble the rifle. None of us believed they were able do this.

The soldier picked up the magazine lying on the porch, put it safely into his pocket, and told the boys that they could give it a try. The boys, who appeared to be about eight or nine years old, sat down in a semicircle and proceeded to break the rifle down into its different component parts. The leader of the group appeared to have more experience. He took the lead in the breakdown. The soldier then pulled out a small rag and wiped down the various parts.

When he was done, the boys started to slowly reassemble the rifle. When the leader had difficulty with the bolt assembly, the boy next to him quickly spoke up and pointed out his mistake. The first boy accepted the advice, made the correct adjustment to the bolt, then continued reassembling the rifle. When they were finished, they handed the weapon back to the soldier. The whole process took less than fifteen minutes. All of us were amazed.

We concluded that they must have watched other passing soldiers clean their weapons, or they had fathers or other relatives in the South Vietnamese army. Their standard weapon was also the M-16, courtesy of Uncle Sam.

That experience would always be one of the hallmarks of a war zone for me, that young children could master the mechanics of firearms before they could master the math and language skills they should be developing. I happened to have my camera with me that day and recorded this ironic scene. We picked up our gear,

Village boys tear down an M-16 for cleaning.

They reassemble the rifle and return it to the GI.

headed out of the village, and spent the rest of the time conducting sweeps over dry land with no VC contact.

At the end of the day on Friday, we'd be on the move again to our newest NDP at the power plant.

# CHAPTER 15

# POWER PLANT

On Saturday, April 19, we went out on an early patrol, and in the afternoon we moved by truck to our new NDP located at the power plant adjacent to Highway 316. The plant was near the Saigon River and provided electric power for large parts of the city of Saigon. The complex consisted of a seven-story building housing much of the equipment and several smaller buildings that contained other items related to power production and distribution. Tall towers supported power lines that led out of the complex and connected to other power lines leading into Saigon.

Our primary mission was to protect the plant from attack. One platoon from our company remained at the plant while the others were out on other missions. In addition to the mortars, there were several banks of launchers for CS gas canisters located on the roof of the main building. In the event of an attack, they could be launched in all four directions from the building to slow down and disorient the enemy.

Our wood-frame hootches had plywood walls and were protected with sandbags on the sides and top. There was running water, so we were happy to learn that we'd get a shower every day. The latrine construction was rather unusual. Fifty-five-gallon drums were cut in half and placed at the base of the latrines. Every two days they were pulled out, and the contents were dumped into a deep nearby pit. Accumulated trash was deposited on top, and the pit was then doused with several gallons of diesel fuel and ignited. The resulting fire burned and sanitized the contents of the pit. This produced a tall black column of smoke sometimes reaching one hundred feet or more into the sky. The plant was so large and well known that there was no attempt to disguise our location. We relied instead on a show of force to deter potential attackers.

An unusual aspect of this NDP was the employment of local civilians to fill sandbags. Every morning about a dozen Vietnamese women arrived for work. They were restricted to one corner of the base and worked slowly and steadily until the late afternoon. A detail of soldiers from our company picked up the filled sandbags and used them to reinforce old hootches and bunkers as well as new structures. This plant was a critical element of the infrastructure of the country; therefore, the defensive measures were stronger than at our previous camps. In other places we were satisfied with a wall of sandbags that were one layer thick. Here the walls were two and in some cases three layers thick. The presence of civilians inside the base was also unusual for us, since most of our base camps were off limits to anyone except US Army and ARVN soldiers.

We set out on a new adventure on Sunday, April 20. We rode trucks to the river and boarded large LSTs, the same type of assault boats used in World War II. Several miles down the river, we cautiously debarked on the riverbank into some pretty thick jungle. We did not face any opposition when the ramp dropped, so we started moving inland along our designated route. We continued on this search and destroy mission all day, then we set up our various ambush sites for the night.

It was a quiet night, and we resumed our patrols the next morning. In the afternoon the LSTs returned and ferried us back to the trucks that took us back to the power plant. It felt good to clean up and get into dry fatigues.

The power plant that provided electricity for Saigon
was our base of operations for two months.

The burn pit at the power plant was used to dispose of trash.

Our platoon sergeant was out of the hospital and back with us, but his leg had not fully healed, so I was still the acting platoon sergeant.

On Tuesday, we boarded helicopters that flew us to a location in a wet muddy field far beyond populated civilian areas. During this time we were receiving our air transportation from a different helicopter unit. At the time, we only knew them by the symbol they painted on the door, which was a white bulldog. As always, we appreciated their service and were always happy to see them. We later learned that they were part of the 129th Assault Helicopter Company.

I brought my camera with me and used the opportunity to record a series of aerial images during our flight over a variety of buildings, hamlets, and rivers. We crossed over a major intersection of two-lane paved highways with new traffic lights. Most of the roads we used were dirt roads or very narrow paved roads. There were motorcycles traveling in both directions on the two highways and several three-wheeled Lambrettas transporting passengers and packages. A local policeman in his white short-sleeve shirt was talking to motorcyclists on the side of the road.

A convoy of empty trucks was turning from one highway onto the other. They appeared to be smaller than US Army trucks, probably belonging to the ARVN forces. Small groups of civilians were walking along the edges of the highway at different points along the way. As our chopper altered its course slightly, we noticed at least seven trucks in the convoy heading away from us. To the right of the convoy, there was a sizable town that stretched for several blocks. The homes were larger and better constructed, with stucco walls and ceramic tile roofs. Our pilot appeared to be following the main road through the town. Along the side of the road, stretching for two blocks was a line of about two hundred people possibly looking for work. The surrounding streets and paths were almost empty. Farther ahead on the left was a large group of people spread out on both sides of the street in a tight cluster next to a long building with an overhang, probably the main marketplace for the town.

We passed over the far edge of the town; the land was flat and devoid of trees and shrubs. We noticed a series of long perfectly aligned low buildings, possibly a factory or military installation. A minute later we saw several rows of trucks and a zigzag pattern of deep trenches lining two sides of the compound. Two separate groups of men were moving along a dirt road in the area below, platoons of soldiers marching to their next project for the day. A bright white guardhouse and gate on the right side of the compound confirmed that this was an ARVN base.

We continued beyond the base and over another village with mostly dirt roads and less densely packed buildings. One of the buildings was quite conspicuous, being almost a block long. It had a large rectangle pool about half the size of the building. There were no items associated with a swimming pool such as diving boards or chairs, so we presumed that the structure was an industrial or agricultural enterprise.

As our aerial tour continued, the buildings grew farther and farther apart. Homes started to give way to large fields formed into perfect squares and rectangles marked by borders of tightly packed earth or berms. The homes disappeared entirely, and the neat fields melded into wild muddy marshes of green grasses. Palm trees lined the irregular borders of the numerous rivers and canals that meandered into the larger river on our left.

As the last vestiges of civilization disappeared, the pilot made an abrupt change in direction and started moving down to a field in the distance. We knew that we were about to land, so we tightened the straps on our helmets and made sure that the magazines in our rifles were snug and secure. I closed the leather cover over my camera and stuck it in the large pocket in my shirt. A Huey gunship had been circling our landing zone, but the gunner was not firing. This was a good sign; it was safe to land. The pilot swooped into the field and allowed the ship to touch the ground lightly for a moment. We rushed out of both sides of the ship, just as he accelerated the rotation of the blades overhead and simultaneously flew forward and upward. At almost the same time, the other helicopters carrying the rest of our platoon touched down. We were ready for another day in the boonies.

It was difficult to make any significant progress due to the extreme heat and the soft, sticky mud underfoot. The strenuous slogging movement was a miserable contrast to the smooth flight we experienced earlier in the air. I was growing tired of these missions. I felt as if I'd been over there all my life, and it was the only world that existed. I was getting dragged out physically and mentally, and I felt a strong need for a long rest, not a two-day rest, but a week or more. I had to quickly realign my thoughts and remember that I was helping to lead this patrol and needed to set a good example.

The army has a term: FE or "false enthusiasm." That day I had to revert to my training and practice FE with everyone around me. It helped all of us to stay focused and safe. I knew I was getting close to leaving this war zone, and I didn't want a dumb mistake to keep me from getting out of there in one piece. We followed our orders, made the best of the situation, and finally made it to the pickup point at the end of the day. The return trip on the helicopters felt like an E ride at Disneyland. It was an exhilarating experience that ended safely.

Christina wrote that a July 19 wedding date would allow her enough time to plan the wedding and still leave the rest of the summer for an extended honeymoon. I enthusiastically agreed and left the arrangements to her.

We tried to keep our hootches at the power plant clean, but a couple of them were bothered by rats that found their way in at night or when no one was around. We had tried a variety of methods to get rid of them but were unsuccessful. After a particularly persistent rat chewed into a parcel from home, one soldier was determined to get rid of it once and for all.

With a knife in one hand and a flashlight in the other, he stood outside his hootch for several nights, looking through the wire screen on the side wall, waiting for the rat to show up. When the culprit finally returned, the soldier excitedly ran in and tried to stab the rat, who unfortunately escaped. Frustrated, he resolved to implement a foolproof solution to the problem.

He got a large piece of cheese from one of the cooks, then took the blasting cap and the wire from a claymore mine and inserted it into the cheese. He placed the cheese in a corner of the hootch under a wooden box held off the ground by a couple of soda cans. He ran the wire outside the hootch and connected it to the plastic hand detonator.

The ambush was set, and he waited patiently in the dark, peering through the screen window for the return of his prey. After an hour or so he heard a rustling noise in the hootch. He looked inside and saw the reflection of light in the rodent's eyes just as it bit into the cheese. He ducked below the screen window and squeezed the detonator. Several soldiers rushed over to check on the noise. He turned on his flashlight, opened the door, and carefully surveyed the damage. He was victorious; he had conquered his enemy.

His victory, however, was not without a cost. A red viscous mess covered portions of the floor, one of the walls, and part of his hootchmate's bunk. As he was cleaning up the mess, his hootchmate returned. He calmed his buddy down and agreed to switch cots with him. His hootch remained rat-free for the next month.

We spent Thursday, April 24, guarding a group of chieu hois (former VC who had gone over to the side of the South Vietnamese government). They were using machetes to cut the palm and heavy growth along riverbanks to eliminate possible ambush sites for the VC. It was similar to the defoliation program that the United States had implemented.

On Friday, our platoon sergeant came back to the field, so another sergeant and I were given the day off. We went to Di An, where I tried to make a call to Christina on the MARS hookup. I waited five hours, but they couldn't get through. Then we checked out a new photo lab they had in Di An. It looked like a big house trailer without windows. It had its own gasoline-operated generator to power the air conditioning and lighting inside. The air conditioner was necessary to maintain the temperature of the various solutions.

We developed a roll of negatives and printed up a batch of pictures. The new lab was a fabulous idea, and I hoped to get a chance to use it again.

More good news. I was getting shorter. Forty-six days left in Vietnam.

On Sunday, April 27, I was sent back to Di An for a couple of days to get some needed parts for our mortars. I also received a letter from Christina letting me know that our wedding date was confirmed for July 19. Now that we had a date, "...just get me to the church on time." For our honeymoon, we decided to enjoy a week at a New England resort before starting our camping trip. Spending a week getting reacquainted with civilization sounded like a good idea to me. I wrote my family about the wedding date and asked my brother Bruce to be my best man. There was a good chance that he'd be going overseas shortly after I was discharged.

While in Di An I tried to call Christina and waited four hours before they could get radio contact with a stateside ham radio. She was out (9:30 a.m., Saturday, NY time), and someone on her end said to call back in two hours. It was not quite that simple. When I got through to New York it was 10:30 p.m. Saturday night in Vietnam. They lost radio contact half an hour later, and I was not able to call back. Besides that, I had to put in a new "patch" (request), and that put me in line behind ten other guys. Discouraged, I went back to the barracks to sleep.

I returned to the MARS office about 07:00 (Sunday in Vietnam) and waited four hours. They picked up a ham radio station in Alaska, but it would be a while before I'd get a chance to call, since there were four guys ahead of me. I was due back in the field at 15:00, so I was hoping that this call would go through. I finally got through to the States in the afternoon (early morning in New York). The phone rang for some time, but no one answered. It would be a couple of weeks before I'd get a chance to call again, but c'est la vie!

On Monday, the choppers picked us up for another monotonous day of patrolling in the mud and flew us to a wet field in the middle of nowhere. Our platoon sergeant, who was wounded, had gone to Lai Khe for a couple of days to get a medal. I was running the platoon again.

Once again, the chopper ride was the best part of the day. We flew over several villages and near the water plant. We also flew over a cemetery with many large tombs that looked bright white from the high altitude. It was next to a narrow dirt road that we had passed through or next to on a number of patrols over the past few months. The terrain below us changed as the homes and roads disappeared, and we headed to a wide expanse of wet fields and palm trees.

The landing zone was a field next to one of the widest places in the river. The familiar water holes created by artillery shells were visible as we approached. We were not sure what to expect, but we did not see any evidence of Viet Cong as we landed. Our platoon formed up and started moving parallel to the river. We continued for a couple of hours without making contact.

Our unit was asked to spend the afternoon covering an area on the other side of the river a couple of kilometers to our left. They were sending engineer boats to meet us. After we broke for lunch, two boats arrived. Half the platoon boarded, while the other half waited for the boats to return. When the entire platoon had reached the other side, we headed out, moving away from the river in the opposite direction.

The palm trees that lined the main river and the smaller tributaries grew thick and tall because of the proximity to water, making our job more difficult. The point man hacked a path through the palm trees with a large machete so that we could pass through. Our movement was slow and arduous, so we changed the point man every thirty minutes. We were in a wild area with no sign of civilization, too far from villages or rice fields. There were plenty of places for an enemy to hide out, and we felt as if we were looking for the proverbial needle in a haystack. In the late afternoon, we received word that we should move to our new pickup point, because the choppers would be inbound in an hour. We reached the site and flew back to our base.

There was an unwritten rule that you got out of the field when you had thirty days left in-country. At this point I had forty-three days left in-country, so I had only thirteen days left in the field.

While in college I worked on the school newspaper, the *Jasper Journal*. I had sent in a story about my experience in Vietnam and included a few photos. They featured my story as the front page lead and included a two-page spread with photos. They mailed me a few copies. I was surprised that they gave the story this much attention, given that the war was even less popular than when I had joined the army two years earlier. I sent copies to my folks and Christina.

We had a stand-down on Wednesday, so I went to the Saigon USO and successfully called my fiancée on a MARS relay. I let her know that I had ordered her ao dai, a red silk dress over white slacks. It would be mailed in two weeks, and I hoped she would like it. We chatted awhile before we had to end the call.

Thursday, May 1, was May Day, and there was a possibility of a Communist offensive, but with forty-one days left I was hoping for a quiet day. It turned out to be a dramatic day. We did not experience a Viet Cong offensive, but while we were on patrol one of the squads spotted three VC about five hundred meters away. We pursued them for over an hour, but they got away. There was always a danger of walking into an enemy ambush, so we tried to move rapidly, but with some caution.

My frustration was mounting with the prospect of going out on another ambush the following night and several more until I would get out of the field. Since we had been concentrating on daytime patrols, I was hoping I would not have to pull another ambush. That was not to be the case.

We set up on Friday night and another platoon blew an ambush about four hundred meters from ours. One man was dusted off for shrapnel wounds in the arm, but it wasn't too serious. Then they brought in artillery, closer than I'd ever seen it, because some of the rounds were landing dangerously near our position.

# CHAPTER 16

# BATTLE OF THE BUFFALO

The adventure continued on Saturday, May 3. Picture a patrol at 18:00 in the evening, moving down a road toward an ambush site. A file of soldiers marched on each side of the road bordered by water on both sides. Suddenly, a water buffalo broke loose from his papa-san and came charging toward the file. It charged and missed one man, who jumped to the side as the buffalo stampeded by. He then headed for the next man and butted him into the water. The soldier's rifle sling hooked around the horns of the buffalo. Now the buffalo had a rifle in his face and was enraged. He charged past me toward a man on the other side of the road. I had a clear shot, aimed my rifle and fired three times, twice in the chest and once in the head, and the buffalo dropped.

We thought that the buffalo had killed the man in the water, because it looked like it got him on its horns. Fortunately, the buffalo hit him with its head, and he was only stunned. We couldn't stop the buffalo sooner, because there was always someone in the line of fire. I was the first one to get a clear shot at him. I had my camera with me, and afterward I took a couple of pictures of a dazed soldier, a peaceful buffalo, and a quizzical papa-san. As soon as the medic confirmed that the soldier hadn't broken anything, we continued moving along the road, eventually reaching our designated location near a river crossing. We set up for the night ambush. The night passed uneventfully, and we returned along the same route in the morning.

As we made our way back to our pickup point, we passed through a small village near the site of the buffalo incident. We noticed that several people carried large chunks of meat dangling from metal hooks. The villagers had cut up and distributed pieces of the buffalo carcass while it was still fresh. The local diet normally consisted of rice and vegetables with an occasional bit of protein from a chicken or a pig. The fresh buffalo meat was a real treat for the villagers. The farmer who owned the buffalo would be able to file a claim with the US Army for the loss of his buffalo and receive compensation to purchase another water buffalo or other livestock. This was one of the more equitable aspects of pacification, where the United States tried to minimize the collateral effects of the war on civilians by providing some compensation for losses.

We get some welcome assistance from the engineers while crossing a wide river.

Still stunned, the man thrown in the water by a charging water buffalo, starts to recover.

The farmer will be compensated by the US Army for the loss of his water buffalo.

The lieutenant sent me into Di An on Sunday to bring back a man who was AWOL. I couldn't find him but learned that he had told everyone he had three days off. I spent the rest of the day in Di An. The truck back to the power plant was late, and I got back a few minutes before my platoon was supposed to leave for a night patrol. The lieutenant told me I didn't have to go out, so I got the night off. It was a good deal!

Everyone was still talking about the buffalo I shot. The guy who shot the buffalo about three months earlier came up to me and said that we were tied one to one. He was now driving a jeep, so I told him that I still might beat him, because I was still out in the field. He said that he might get one with his jeep yet, so we'd still be even.

In one of her letters, Christina asked how I felt about the "experience" of being in Vietnam. I told her that it was complicated and difficult to explain in a letter, and I'd be better able to describe it when I got back to the States. But one thing I had learned was that Communism *was* real, not some vague mirage that threatened the dreams of some conservative politician. I had seen Russian bullets, Russian rifles, Russian mortars, and Chinese grenades.

MSU sent a letter stating that they had not received copies of the scores from the Graduate Record Exam that I had taken a couple of years earlier. I notified the exam center in New Jersey and requested that they send the scores. I was not overly concerned about making a September enrollment date but wanted to finalize my school plans, since my army career was coming to an end.

On Monday, May 5, we had a pretty quiet night on ambush. I was looking forward to the next night's operation on PBRs—the same type of patrol boat we had used a few weeks earlier. I always liked missions that involved boats. When I look back, I think I probably should have joined the navy.

Unfortunately, the operation was changed, and we were trucked out to our mission. C'est la guerre. It was a very busy night. Our company set up in several sites close to ours. Three ambushes were blown; one of them was only a few hundred meters from our position. We were not sure if any VC were killed or wounded in any of these actions. That was one of the big frustrations of this war. We'd fire at them, and they'd fire at us, and then they'd disappear, probably the ultimate definition of a guerrilla war. I felt that I had been very lucky so far with indirect enemy contact of very short engagements lasting ten to fifteen minutes. The fighting had been much more direct farther up north. Our company's casualty rate was much lower than I had expected.

When we got back in the morning, we found out that they had shown *Doctor Zhivago*, about two people who were very much in love despite the background of an all-encompassing war. Christina and I had seen it when it was first released, and it was one of our favorites.

The next day we headed to our drop-off point, riding in trucks along a new route. We drove through a town past a large Catholic church, surrounded by a freshly painted white fence. Above the entrance was a tall steeple. Many people were going in and out of the church. Next to the church was a huge grotto, almost 150 feet high, built of black-and-gray concrete resembling the side of a rocky hill. The left side of the grotto was in shadows, but the sun shone brightly on the statue of Mary that rested near the top of the grotto opening. The white statue was in sharp contrast to the dark colors of the grotto. A few people were praying on the steps at the base of the grotto.

The scene was another example of the incongruity of the war. The worshipers in this church were looking for solace and some meaning in their lives, and we were heading out on a patrol to find and perhaps kill other "enemy" soldiers. It was possible that these other soldiers were relatives of the people praying in this church.

As we continued down the road, I was standing on the bed of the truck near the front and looking down on the driver in the open cab. I noticed that the gear shift knob was missing. The driver had replaced it with a "field expedient," i.e., a screwdriver handle. It was a simple and effective fix. The maintenance crew in the motor pool could have filled out a requisition for the shift knob and might have been waiting for one to be shipped. In the meantime, the screwdriver handle solved the immediate problem.

The army heartily encouraged the use of field expedients. It was part of training courses for just about every MOS specialty in the army. The soldier was taught to think about alternative uses for every tool and object available in a given situation. In this way, a chunk of C-4 explosive could be ignited with a match and used to cook food. A sheet of clear plastic from an ammunition crate could be used to make a clear, yet waterproof window in a hootch. The elastic band that held a camouflage cover on a helmet became a place to store cigarettes or papers that a soldier wanted to keep dry.

As our convoy continued, our trip became more interesting. We were now on one of the few four-lane highways in Vietnam, consisting of two lanes heading toward Saigon and two more heading away from the city. We noticed a number of small impromptu roadside stands made up of a single table or a small platform attached to a bicycle. Many of them had tarps attached overhead for a bit of shade. Most were selling a single product, such as melons or coconuts. We often saw the drivers of motorcycles and Lambrettas stop and negotiate the price of the products, so they must have been in demand. The American capitalism model seemed to be alive and well.

As we drove through a small town, we saw an ice cart making deliveries. The cart was an oversize bicycle with one wheel, the seat and handlebars at the rear, and a metal frame cart resting on an axle with two wheels in the front. The cart held seven long blocks of ice about one foot wide and four feet long. This was the first time I had seen civilians with the large blocks of ice. The ice was kept in metal or wooden coolers that served as iceboxes in homes and businesses without refrigerators or electricity. We had seen young boys standing outside the gates of some of our base camps selling cold Cokes from small Styrofoam coolers filled with chunks of ice. I now understood where the young vendors had gotten their ice.

Farther along the road, several motorbikes were lined up to purchase one or two liters of gasoline at an Esso station. It was the first Esso station I had seen in Vietnam. Most sold Shell gasoline.

We passed a large rubber plantation on the left side of the convoy. It was easy to recognize because of the tall narrow trees planted with care in long uniform rows to provide easy access to the natural rubber.

We turned off the highway and proceeded along a narrow two-lane road heading away from the heavily populated areas toward the wilder and wetter lands where we would begin our mission. We passed an unusual military vehicle moving in the opposite direction. Our driver slowed down to wave to the crew of this strange vehicle that we had not seen before.

It was similar to an APC, having the same tracks and the same general boxlike shape, but on the top of the vehicle there were long twin .50-caliber barrels protruding from the metal shield in the center turret. The turret looked like it was able to swivel left and right to provide a wide field of fire. There was a separate M-60 machine gun mounted farther back on the left side of the top deck of the vehicle.

We learned that it was a version of the M-113-ACAV, a personnel carrier modified to take on a more aggressive role. Rather than protecting infantry inside the vehicle, it was designed to go after enemy positions with more firepower. The dark-green metal shield at the center was painted with white letters proclaiming "Aggressors II" and "Hired Guns." The crew had personalized the vehicles to let other American units know that they were proud of their machines and eager for a fight. Just how deeply the individual soldiers on the vehicle really believed this was hard to tell. Some of them may truly have wanted to test their vehicle's prowess in a firefight, while the others may have been silently hoping that just the appearance of the menacing machine would deter an enemy from starting a fight in the first place. We didn't have time to get an answer from the crew, because we had passed them and had reached our destination. We dismounted and headed out on foot to meet the objectives of our own mission.

On Wednesday, May 7, I received some very bad news. It was announced in our platoon that no one would stand-down until seven days prior to his date of leaving country. Nevertheless, I was still planning on getting out of the field thirty days prior, even if it meant a court-martial. They could bust me and take some money away, but I didn't believe they could extend my tour in the army. I was hoping it wouldn't come to that, but I was too close to going home in one piece to continue taking chances. It never came to that.

One of the other sergeants clued me in that the seven-day stand-down announcement was a joke for my benefit, because the lieutenant thought I looked too eager to leave.

We set out on another patrol and were in the mud all day. At 12:30 the monsoon season officially began. It started pouring and rained for hours. I was glad to be getting out of the field very soon.

Friday, May 9, was *a great day!* Officially, it was my last day in the field. We wound up spending a lot of time moving through a wide river. We were wet much of the day, but it did not matter to me. It was my last helicopter ride. It was my last river crossing. It was my last patrol through the mud and crud. It was the last lunch eaten from tin cans while looking out for VC. It was truly a great day!

When I got back that night, I received even better news. My new orders stated that I would be leaving Vietnam on June 7, 1969. Instead of flying to Fort Ord, California, I would be flying to Fort Dix, New Jersey. I was supposed to be discharged on June 18, but since I was going back early, I might be discharged a couple of days earlier. I wouldn't know until I got there.

On Sunday, May 11, I made a MARS call to my mother for Mother's Day, but the radio connection was very poor, and I could barely hear her. I told her about my new orders and the date when I would be leaving Vietnam.

I also received a letter from my brother Bruce, who was in training for MOS 31E at the radio repair school. I sent him a detailed letter.

"I received your letter today about your Vietnam levy for June at Fort Dix. I would like you to be my best man if at all possible. I was talking to the first sergeant in our company, and he said you have a good chance of making my wedding. He said you should: 1. Send a copy of your orders; 2. State that you are best man at my wedding; 3. State that we want to see each other after being separated for a year; 4. Request a leave extension or a delay on your departure date; 5. Send all this to the sergeant major of the army, Department of the Army, Washington, DC.

The author's final patrol in the field, as the mortar
platoon moves cautiously through a river.

We passed an M-113-ACAV with Twin .50s and an
M-60 while on our way to an ambush site.

"You can check with your first sergeant or an army chaplain first, and they might help you cut through some red tape...

"...If you see Elaine, offer her my congratulations on becoming a nurse. I received my orders yesterday, and I will be arriving at Fort Dix on June 8, 1969, to process out for discharge. You might be getting on the plane that I get off. Write me a letter and let me know how things work out."

I now had twenty-six days left in Vietnam. *Short!*

It was Monday, May 12. I wasn't in the field, and I was very happy about it. Everyone else got up at 05:30 and left at 06:30. I got up at 06:30 and still managed to catch breakfast. The day started out very warm. It became cloudy in the afternoon, and then the rain started and helped things to cool off. It rained fairly regularly now, and it was nice to sit in my hootch until the rain stopped. I spent most of my days stacking sandbags and building bunkers. They were pretty easy days, with long breaks.

On Wednesday, I received an audiotape from Christina. I borrowed a cassette tape player from a friend of mine, Spec-4 Jones in supply. The tape had obviously been recorded in the middle of a family party, where there was lots of laughter and a fair amount to drink. Her family was very fun-loving, especially her older brothers. I enjoyed listening to the Cold Spring Harbor Trio singing "Prisoner of Love." Then her sister-in-law, Sheila, sang the Irish ballad "Will Ye Go Lassie (Laddie) Go?" It was really special. Some of the guys were listening and asked me to replay her song several times. Christina's other sister-in-law, Jane, also gave a beautiful a cappela performance of "Irish Soldier Boy." I felt like I was already part of the family!

Later in the evening they showed two movies, *You Only Live Twice* and *Tony Rome*. Life was definitely improving.

Christina sent a letter telling me that the call I had made on Mother's Day to my mom actually went to her instead. The connection was so bad that I hadn't recognized her voice. Her number was listed as an alternate, and they called her when my mother's number didn't answer. The incident became even funnier, because I had sent a letter to my mother the next day saying that I enjoyed talking with her and Gary on the phone. Christina said that she called my mom right after my call when she realized what happened. The whole incident was hilarious.

We had a hectic day on Saturday, May 17. I was gassed for the umpteenth time during my army career. We had a load of sandbags to move, so we borrowed a truck and trailer from an army engineer unit near us. We were loading the bags when we suddenly started breaking out in tears and coughing. I looked in the trailer and saw a broken sack containing persistent CS gas (tear gas) in powder form. It was a nonlethal gas that worked primarily as an irritant. They used it to discourage VC from reentering tunnels that had been cleared out. I took it out of the truck, dug a hole, and buried it.

We found out that our platoon was on a special extended operation building a new NDP in the boonies. The next night they took two of our mortars out to the field. We then loaded a truck with several hundred rounds of mortar ammo as well as mail, food, and water which was headed to the NDP.

Tuesday was spent working on the bunker we'd been building. The platoon was still out at the new NDP. They were supposed to be there for two more days, but I guessed it would be longer. The first sergeant wanted me to go out to the NDP to help. Fortunately, I had a dentist appointment the next day, so I had an excuse for not going. The NDP wasn't that bad, but not as secure as the power plant. I was not required to go on patrols and did not want to take any chances with only three weeks left in Vietnam.

On Thursday, May 22, I reluctantly went out to the location where my platoon had been building the bunkers. They were actually scheduled to leave that NDP, and when I got there, they were in the process of leveling the place. I helped take down the radar tower, dismantle the bunkers, and load sandbags on trucks. The whole thing was some sort of experiment to see how fast a new NDP could be set up and taken down.

No mail came on Friday. It rained most of the day and into the evening. My platoon went out on ambush, and I honestly did not miss spending nights trying to sleep on a rainy berm. The bunker that we'd been building for some time now was almost completed. I was just counting the days.

# CHAPTER 17

# VUNG TAU

While in Vietnam you were entitled to one R&R and a three-day pass. I went in to Di An on May 26, to get ready for my three-day pass for Vung Tau, an army-run resort on the coast on the South China Sea, about twenty-five miles southwest of Saigon.

They offered me a pass two weeks before my R&R in January, but I had turned it down, because the dates were too close together. The first sergeant had been hassling me about rescheduling it for several months, so I mentioned it during a meeting with the captain when I was running the platoon. At that time, I was getting short, and I wanted the pass before going home. It finally came through. The resort was secure, because there were several infantry units guarding the perimeter and eight-inch artillery pieces plus navy patrol boats guarding the beach. The room and food were free if you stayed at the army R&R center, although you could also stay at one of several Vietnamese hotels.

On Tuesday morning, May 27, I headed over to the small airfield on the base at Di An with about other twenty guys also traveling to Vung Tau. One of the other passengers was a South Korean army officer, who agreed to let me take his picture. The Koreans were one of our stronger allies, and they had an excellent reputation for being tough fighters. The acronym for these troops was ROK, Republic of Korea. Everyone called them ROKs, but it was used as a term of respect.

The Caribou was a twin-engine prop plane with a high tail section that rose above the rest of the fuselage. It also featured a cargo ramp that dropped down from the belly so that people and cargo could enter from the rear of the craft. There were several of these on the ground taxiing around the flight line. I was fascinated by the shape of these strange-looking crafts and shot half a roll of film of the planes and the soldiers waiting to take off. Our turn finally came to board, and as I left the terminal area to approach the plane, I saw a large sign, "Absolutely No Picture Taking Of/ On the Flight Line." I snapped one last picture of the sign then stashed the camera in my travel bag. I was not planning to send copies of the pictures to the VC, but MPs were not known for their understanding.

We boarded the aircraft and learned that we were guests of the US Air Force. A yellow sign was painted on the forward bulkhead, "486 Tactical Airlift Wing, 537 Tactical Air Squadron—Welcome Aboard." It was actually a short flight to Vung Tau, since it wasn't that far from Saigon, but the views outside the plane were impressive: dragon-shaped rivers with serpentine paths through the fields and jungles. Then we climbed higher to allow the plane to clear the first mountains I had seen in this country. The landing was smooth and uneventful.

Vung Tau was an air base, an army depot, and a navy port. It was surrounded on three sides by extremely steep and beautiful mountains, and it was easy to defend once you secured the high ground. We could see why the VC didn't bother this place.

I understood that there was a photo lab operated by the Army Special Services, so I had brought a batch of negatives with me. I checked in at the R&R Center, and then went to the photo lab. The place was well equipped, with six enlargers (no waiting). I printed

120 eight-by-ten black-and-white prints. The lab normally closed at 20:30, but I explained to the specialist in charge that our photo lab was not working due to a faulty generator, so he let me finish the job. The pictures were for men in our company who had asked me to make copies of photos of them in action in the field. I had a ball and finished up at 22:00.

It felt great wearing civilian clothes. I had a dinner of army chow in the R&R dining room. However, unlike the mess hall, the chairs were comfortable, and a Vietnamese waitress wearing an ao dai presented me a menu with six choices of meals. She served the food and kept my glass filled with beer. There was no tipping. Outside, a Vietnamese band was playing American songs, and the area was lit up with colored lanterns. Mixed drinks were twenty-five cents. The next day I planned to go downtown and have a look at the local scenery.

The next morning, I enjoyed a great breakfast in the dining room, grabbed my camera and several rolls of film, and headed out on foot to enjoy the sights and sounds of this "tourist" town. I came upon several restaurants that served the local Vietnamese population as well as American servicemen. One of the restaurants had a sign with a large picture of Mickey Mouse pointing out the specials of the day in Vietnamese. We had seen numerous businesses using Disney characters, including Donald Duck and Mickey Mouse, to attract the attention of GIs to shops and restaurants throughout Vietnam. I seriously doubted that these enterprising entrepreneurs had bothered with the formality of paying the Disney Corporation licensing fees for the commercial use of these images. I also doubted that Disney spent very much time or money trying to collect these fees in Vietnam, but I could be wrong.

The sign on the restaurant next to Mickey Mouse also tried to appeal to the GIs' taste for familiar food. They proudly offered hamburgers and "sandwitches" (sic). A short distance away was another stand piled high with loaves of French bread next to a small glass case with large rolls of meat—salami, bologna, and ham, and a plate of large pickles. The woman offered to hand slice some deli meat and place it on a fresh-cut loaf of bread. The case was not refrigerated, but at least it kept the flies off the meat. Apparently, most of her customers were not concerned about the lack of refrigeration. I passed on the sandwich. With only a short time left in-country, I didn't want to take a chance on food poisoning or dysentery extending my stay involuntarily.

The next vendor had a small sign on the front of his cart proclaiming, "nước mía." I had seen this product being sold in many villages during some of my patrols. He operated a fresh sugar cane press. A three-foot stalk of sugar cane was placed between two rolling metal drums. The sweet juice was squeezed out and drained to a funnel that poured it into a glass. Most of the presses that I had come across were operated by a hand crank, but this vendor had attached a small electric motor that pressed the juice more quickly.

A different vendor operated one of the ubiquitous tobacco shops located throughout the country. It was simply a small wooden table with small stacks of familiar brands of cigarettes: Marlboro, Camel, Winston, Lucky Strike, and Salem. Salem had the reputation of being the favorite of most of the male Vietnamese smokers. We all had a pretty good idea of the source of the cigarettes. They didn't come from the normal wholesalers as in most countries. These cigarettes made their way to the market through a barter arrangement between soldiers who received them in SP packs or purchased them at heavily discounted prices at the PX. The cigarettes were used to purchase beer, soda, haircuts, and a variety of other services. The Vietnamese government issued dongs and piasters while the US military issued MPC as currency, but the most common currency was often American cigarettes.

The center of the daily open-air market consisted of a series of covered stalls set up shortly after dawn. The vendors offered a wide variety of vegetables, fruit, meat, fish, and bread. There were large baskets of eggs, carrots, cabbage, pineapple, onions, limes, and several vegetables that I didn't recognize. One of the vendors was selling fresh meat. Chickens and pigs had been cut up into small pieces weighing from half a pound to a pound each. The meat was laid out on a layer of wax paper on a plain wooden counter top. The meat was neither covered nor refrigerated, but it looked fresh and was probably safe to eat if taken home and cooked immediately for the large midday meal. I wondered if the vendor packed the unsold meat in ice to sell the next day, since ice was available in this city. Electricity was also available, so the vendor might even have a refrigerator to store the meat until returning to the market the next morning.

"Fresh" was definitely the word to describe the market. Another woman was selling fish. She removed four black fish from a large aluminum tub filled with what appeared to be river water and transferred the fish (eight to ten inches long) to a smaller aluminum pan. The fish were flopping around inside the pan. A customer nodded yes to the vendor as she prepared to pay for the fish. The whole scene was fascinating, because my experience with seafood was seeing lifeless fish sitting in display cases in supermarkets in the United States. The other interesting aspect was the use of the aluminum pans. I wondered if they were more of the recycled aluminum flares that had been repurposed to serve as food containers.

It was almost noon, and the market was closing. A woman with a balance scale separated the pans from the chains and folded up her scale. A young girl disassembled the wood-frame poles that supported a plastic cover over her stall. The plastic covers on all the stalls were the same army ponchos that we used. The opening for the head was sewn shut to keep out the sun and the rain.

After the market closed in the open street, we were better able to see the more permanent shops along the sidewalks. A jewelry shop had a large glass case filled with rings, bracelets, and necklaces. A few were gold or gold-plated, but most must have been made with silver or silver alloy because the prices were very affordable. Business was slow; there were few customers. On the other hand, the shop next door was packed with customers. It was a combination pool hall and foosball arcade. Foosball was similar to soccer and played on a small table with two to five rigid figures fastened to a long rod that extended outside the table. Groups of kids, ten to fourteen years old, monopolized the tables, energetically rotating the rods to kick the tiny balls into the goal. It was very popular among young boys and may have been introduced by the French years earlier. The French term for the game was something akin to "baby foot."

Another building resembling a motel had the flags of Australia and New Zealand mounted in front, next to a South Vietnamese flag. The sign above the flags read, "AFV (Australian Force Vietnam) Amenities and Welfare Unit, R&C Detachment." The R&C refers to rest and convalescence and was similar to the US Army's R&R centers. It was a reminder of the presence of two allies who had joined the United States in this conflict.

Early on Thursday, I took a pony cart ride to the Thich Ca Phat Dai Pagoda on the top of a mountain to see a giant statue of Buddha. Formed of white concrete, Buddha sat on a lotus blossom with eyes closed and hands joined together in his lap. A young boy told me to remove my shoes as I approached the statue. There was a small multicolored flag near the base of the statue like the one we had seen while on patrol at the Buddhist monastery several weeks earlier. The view from the temple was impressive; the Buddha overlooked the beach and harbor in Vung Tau. It was a cloudy day, but I got some great pictures.

After taking a number of photos, I left the temple and returned by pony cart to the center of Vung Tau. I was anxious to get in a swim, so I headed over to the Beachcomber Club, also operated by

Army Special Services. It was surrounded by a cement wall topped with a barbed-wire fence. After passing the guard at the entrance, I joined a couple of GIs from another unit on the open-air patio where they were serving food and drinks.

After lunch, I headed to the beach. The water was warm, and the view was spectacular! Servicemen were relaxing on blankets on the sand along with a few civilians. Some of the guys shared their blankets with young Vietnamese women. Several vendors walked along the beach offering a variety of food items and souvenirs. One young lady carried a basket of fresh pineapples and artistically carved them up for a small price. She started by removing the outer skin then carved the fruit in a thin spiral pattern which made it look very appetizing. One of the soldiers paid her for the pineapple, and she moved on to other people on the beach. After a long swim, I changed and walked along the road to a group of fishing boats at the far end of the beach.

As I walked along the beach road and looked out across the South China Sea, I saw two or three large vessels in the distance that appeared to be navy ships and commercial cargo ships. Closer in, I saw about forty or fifty smaller fishing boats anchored very close to the beach. It was low tide, and there were another dozen boats sitting on the sand, waiting for the tide to return. Most of the wooden vessels were between twenty and thirty feet long. A few had a mast for a sail, but most were powered by motors. The shoreline had a very long and gradual slope, providing plenty of places to moor boats or beach them. A laborer was repairing a dented propeller blade under a boat resting on its side. He was banging it back into shape with a hammer and mallet, while two others were helping to stabilize the boat. A fourth used a metal scraping tool to remove marine growth from the bottom of the hull.

Another craftsman used a large axe to make rough cuts in a long piece of angled wood that he was shaping into a rib for the inside of an old boat. He had already finished one rib and had smoothed the edges with a handsaw. Most of these fishermen were using hand tools to repair and maintain their boats in the same manner that they had done for many years. Power tools would have been quicker and more efficient, but the cost and availability were probably limiting factors.

Young men carried supplies and gear through the surf out to the boats that were in the water. Four teenage boys stood next to two oversize baskets constructed with tightly woven grass or leaves. They were about six feet across and three or four feet high with rounded bottoms. At first I thought that they were small boats that could be paddled short distances between the shore and boats close to shore, but I realized that they were containers designed to hold and transport the fish caught farther out at sea.

A Caribou aircraft flies to the resort town of Vung Tau,
courtesy of the 537th Tactical Air Squadron.

Fishing boats rest in the sand at Vung Tau. They would
head out to fish with the morning tide.

The sky started to darken, and a typical afternoon storm was developing. The sea started to churn, and black clouds alternated with rays of sunshine. I took a series of photos of the fishing boats bouncing around in the turbulent water. The skies opened up, and I was suddenly drenched. I closed up my camera and walked back to the R&R center. Even though I was wet, I didn't feel very cold. I had spent many afternoons walking through jungles and rice paddies with no control over how long or how far I would have to go. Today, I was a tourist, and I was able to end the discomfort with a dry towel after capturing some very dramatic and satisfying photos.

On my last night in Vung Tau, I decided to check out the night life. I didn't have far to go, because the R&R center had a Vietnamese group performing in the courtyard on an outdoor stage. The group was named Choice 69, implying that they played the best music of 1969. It featured five male musicians and two female backup singers.

As they played and sang a variety of American songs from the six-ties, it became apparent that English was not their first language, and they were singing the lyrics phonetically. It didn't matter, be-cause it was great to hear familiar music performed live. Besides, there was no cover charge, and the drinks at the center were inex-pensive. A couple dozen GIs were watching the group and enjoy-ing the drinks. After an hour of snapping some pictures, I headed downtown with a couple of other guys to see the city at night.

We were surprised to see many of the shops, bars, and restau-rants cheerfully lit up with colored lights. The shops selling souve-nirs had open fronts with well-lit interiors and display cases with fluorescent lights that illuminated the Vietnamese dolls, ceramic elephants, and wooden jewelry boxes. Every other village and town that we encountered at night or dusk went dark at sundown except for a few dim lights in the homes. This was the first town in Vietnam where I had seen lights at night since arriving almost a year ago.

Groups of GIs were standing or sitting at tables in front of sev-eral bars, and we visited a couple. We came upon the strange sight of two Americans in civilian clothes squatting on their knees try-ing to pet a German shepherd that a dog handler had brought into the bar. The meeting was amicable, and the handler and the dog seemed to relish the attention. Most of the handlers that I had met discouraged other people from touching their dogs or giving them too much attention. It was also the first time I became aware that the dogs received an in-country R&R trip to Vung Tau. Did the dogs also receive a choice of Hawaii, Australia, or Hong Kong for a longer R&R visit?

We stopped at another bar and sat down at a table. Several host-esses employed by the bar joined us at the table and asked us to buy them a "Saigon tea." The tea was overpriced and cost the same as a glass of hard liquor, but we knew that they would sit and chat with us for about fifteen minutes before we'd be encouraged to buy them another. We had agreed ahead of time to order three teas and three beers. We talked for a short time then decided to leave before needing to order more tea. I took a few pictures to commemorate the evening. The other two guys continued barhopping, but I headed back to the R&R center.

We left early on Friday and flew back on another Caribou aircraft. It was a great trip, and I was thankful for the opportunity to take a minivacation with Uncle Sam picking up the tab. I was now ready to focus on the final days before leaving Vietnam.

# CHAPTER 18

# FINAL DAYS

I rode the supply truck back to the power plant. When I arrived, a letter was waiting. My brother's request for a leave extension came through, and his port call had been changed from June 17 to July 22. He wrote me saying, "So I'll be proud to be your best man." What a great piece of news!

As my time in Vietnam was drawing to a close, I reflected on the events of the past year. It had been and will remain the most challenging and transformational year of my life. I arrived a naïve and anxious individual to face the daily boredom, drudgery, and occasional intensity of combat and was leaving as a sergeant with the sober memories of wounded and dead companions, who were not as fortunate as me. I felt that I had been very lucky. Numerous members of our company were killed or wounded over the past twelve months. Four men in our company of two hundred lost their lives during my tour, a 2 percent casualty rate. Other companies in our division and companies in other areas of Vietnam experienced much higher casualty rates. There were many times when I could have been injured by being in the wrong place at the wrong time. On some of those patrols, I could have been hurt simply by walking a little faster or a little slower. The randomness of chance assigned me to a "lucky" unit. The randomness of chance placed me on patrols when there was no contact and placed me in the camp when there was contact. I considered my time in Vietnam to be one of the luckiest times of my life. I tried to view each day of my life after that as a special gift. I also tried to embrace new challenges with a greater degree of self-confidence and frequently asked myself, "What's the worst that can happen?" The worst case in most situations was not nearly as bad as the consequences of risks that I had been taking there.

On Saturday, May 31, I packed up all of my personal gear and said good-bye to my friends in the mortar platoon and other members of the company. The eight-by-ten photos were a parting gift. I boarded the supply truck and headed to the main base camp at Di An.

I arrived in Di An and reported to the barracks where I had begun my tour. I stayed there until my departure date. It was pretty easy duty: some minor cleanup details during the day and guard duty at night. I was the NCO in charge of guard duty, but it was one night on and two nights off.

I received two letters from Christina on Sunday, June 1. She asked about the details of my arrival, but I didn't have that information. All I knew was that on June 7, I was scheduled to leave Vietnam and fly to Fort Dix. I told her not to plan on seeing me before June 10, so she wouldn't be disappointed. After a year overseas, I was anxious to go home, but I'd go nuts trying to figure out exactly when I'd be leaving, because I knew how changeable and unpredictable the army could be.

Christina mentioned that her sister, Jean, and husband, Tom, were looking forward to meeting me if by chance I stopped in San Francisco. I told her that it was unlikely.

With six days left, I packed some more gear and went to the USO in Di An to see *Hell Fighters* with John Wayne. I was getting very *short!*

On Monday, June 2, I sent a big box of personal gear home. It had my civilian glasses in it, so if it arrived late, I'd be sporting my army glasses a bit longer.

I wrote my final letters to my family and Christina. "This is to be my last letter to you written from the Big Rice Paddy. I started processing today and got three shots (smallpox, plague, and cholera), and I signed out of my company. See you all next week. I want you to know also that I have deeply appreciated all the letters and packages this past year. They meant a lot to me. After a year over here, I wish you to remember me with love, Steve."

I printed the following message on the back of the envelope.

## SHORT!!! Three days, then Xin Loi![4]

I rode on the supply truck for a laundry run to Thu Duc along with a couple of other soldiers. On the way there, we passed an ARVN training base. There was an outdoor session underway, most likely tactics or a similar subject. The instructor had a large chalkboard resting on an easel under a wide-branched tree. About twenty trainees in freshly starched fatigues listened attentively. It was somehow reassuring to see South Vietnamese soldiers going through the training that was similar to our experience in the States.

We completed the laundry run and headed back to camp in the early afternoon. I returned to the default job of every infantry soldier at any base camp—filling sandbags! There was a certain satisfaction in being able to see the result of one's labor, looking at a neat stack of sandbags at the end of the day and saying, "I filled these." The future would hold other jobs for me, requiring more mental work in the form of strategic planning and communicating with business associates and customers. Some of those days would be frustrating, and I would question whether my work efforts had made much difference. At those times I would think back to my days in the army and wish that I had a nice neat stack of sandbags to quantify a day's work.

---

4   "Xin loi" is Vietnamese for "Sorry about that." In this context, it's meant as an ironic way to say good-bye, i.e., *not* really sorry about leaving the war zone.

Happy soldiers line up on the tarmac at Tan Son Nhut Air Base for
a seat on the "Freedom Bird" and a flight back to the States.

The author meets Jean for the first time on his return from Vietnam.

On Friday, June 6, I received a new set of orders. Bad news, good news! Instead of flying out on June 7 and being discharged on June 18, I would now fly out on Tuesday, June 10, and be discharged on June 11. The bottom line was that I'd stay in Vietnam three extra days but be released from active duty seven days earlier. It was good news and looked like a final set of orders, so I hoped that the dates would stick.

The change of orders now meant that I would be flying to California instead of New Jersey. I was scheduled to arrive at Travis Air Force Base on Tuesday, June 10, and then be transported to Oakland Army Base for final processing and discharge on June 11. I would now have the opportunity to visit Jean and Tom in San Francisco while I was in California!

The Freedom Bird arrived on Tuesday, June 10, at Tan Son Nhut Air Base in Saigon. It was a TWA charter flight from Vietnam to California. The mood among my fellow GIs was jubilant. As the plane rolled up to our loading area, it became clear that the role of the passengers had been reversed. The door of the plane opened and a steady stream of incoming GIs in Class A khaki uniforms descended and grimly walked across the tarmac. When they finally passed, we, dressed in standard green fatigues, started moving forward and boarded the plane.

We were thrilled to be on the plane and eager to fly to a safer life. The doors closed, and the pilot started the engines. We taxied down the runway and took off. Many of us were still cautious, well aware that a planeload of GIs was still an inviting target, and we were still in range for small arms fire as well as rockets. After a few more minutes had passed, the pilot finally announced that we had cleared Vietnamese airspace. A cheer went up as we realized that we were finally on the way home!

We made refueling stops at Kadena Air Base in Okinawa and Hawaii. We left Vietnam at 10:15 a.m. on June 10 and arrived at

Travis Air Force Base in California at 5:55 a.m. on June 10 because of the magic of the International Date Line.

The schedule of flight times and refueling stops is one I will remember for the rest of my life.

Leave Vietnam 10:15 Jun 10
Arrive Okinawa 13:50

Leave Okinawa 15:15
Arrive Hawaii 23:40

Leave Hawaii 01:10 Jun 10 (crossed International Date Line)
Arrive Travis AFB 05:55

When we arrived at Travis, buses were waiting to take us to Oakland Army Base. There were no bands to greet us, but we didn't care. We were exhausted after the long flight and wanted to get through the next series of steps and go home. Just inside the door of the large processing building, there was a giant white sign with red, white, and blue lettering: "Welcome home, soldier. USA is proud of you."

At the first of many stations in the building, we were given a quick overview of the steps that we needed to complete before discharge. Some of us were ending our army career in the building. Others were going on leave and would then report to a new stateside duty station.

We had a choice of a two-day process from 8:00 a.m. to 5:00 p.m. or process throughout the night with discharge early the next morning Wednesday, June 11. I chose to go straight through. I did take a short break and called Jean and Tom, letting them know that I had arrived in Oakland. We agreed to meet in San Francisco the next day.

I spent the next twenty-four hours filling out a variety of forms, receiving a medical exam and a new dress uniform. I also met with a Veterans Administration counselor who explained my rights under the GI Bill, including home loan options and educational benefits. I was especially interested in the latter to help cover tuition and other expenses for grad school in September. We took breaks for meals in the mess hall on the base and short naps while waiting for our names to be called at required paperwork stations. We were not happy about the time and detail required but understood that for some of us, this would be our final day in the army, and we'd be free to get on with our lives.

The next morning I drew my final pay and received a plane ticket back to New York! I quickly left the building and took a bus to San Francisco. I was wearing a new dress-green uniform with crisp new sergeant stripes and several ribbons and medals. I was not sure what each of the ribbons represented, but I would look them up later in the large discharge folder they gave us. Jean and Tom picked me up at the bus stop in San Francisco, and I got a quick tour of the city before going to their apartment.

They had lived in California for some time, and I never had the opportunity to meet them while dating Christina. They were both warm and friendly, and Jean looked a lot like Christina, so I felt at home already. She was eight months pregnant and definitely had the glow of a new mother. We drove across the Golden Gate Bridge to take a few pictures of the three of us with San Francisco in the background. Tom made a dinner reservation at the Spinnaker in Sausalito. Dinner was magnificent, complete with a view of the bay and the city! I spent the night at their apartment and slept soundly on a real bed.

The next morning they drove me to San Francisco International Airport, and we said good-bye at the United Airlines gate for the final leg of my journey home. It was a smooth flight across the country. It was a clear sunny afternoon as we approached JFK

Airport. The plane began a long slow pass over Breezy Point and the Rockaways and gently landed.

I was still wearing my dress-green uniform when I walked down the ramp. There was a large group of people waiting to greet the passengers. I noticed a smaller group pointing at me, but I didn't recognize them. Then I saw Christina standing there with a beautiful smile on her face. We embraced, kissed, and she said, "Welcome home." It was a great feeling to finally be back home. As we left the airport, she explained that there was a large Italian family waiting for a relative on my plane. While in the waiting area, she was sitting next to the grandmother, who asked her who she was meeting. When Christina mentioned that I was returning from Vietnam, the woman became very excited. She and her family stood up and were eagerly waiting for me to come down the ramp and kiss her. The crowd was not as large as the Times Square crowd in that famous "kiss" photo at the end of World War II, but the kiss was just as emotional for me. My war was over.

# EPILOGUE

The wedding went off as planned. Christina and I were married in July. My brother Bruce was my best man, and my brother Gary was the head usher. Bruce headed to Vietnam a few days after the wedding and spent a year with HHD, Signal Support Agency, in Long Binh repairing radios. He returned safely, and I was able to attend his wedding when he married Elaine, a navy nurse.

Christina and I spent six weeks on an extended honeymoon/camping trip, traveling from New York City through New England, north to Nova Scotia, and then west to Michigan. Our honeymoon started out on a memorable note, because we were able to watch the moon landing the day after we were married.

I was accepted at Michigan State University for the MBA program that September. The war continued to have an impact on my consciousness. There was a field of white crosses on the MSU campus that represented the rising toll of American lives. I joined the student veterans' group on campus and attended a number of social functions, where we shared some of our experiences, but the war remained an extremely unpopular subject, and most students and friends did not want to hear about it.

When I finally had the opportunity to look at the slides that I had taken during my year in the Big Rice Paddy, it was an amazing experience to view them and remember the circumstances surrounding each image. I chose the best of the slides and filled twelve slide carousels with the pictures. I showed the slides to close friends and family members for a few years and then stored them away.

The extra slides, along with several shoe boxes full of black-and-white photos and negatives, continued to remain in storage, unopened for more than forty years. After grad school I was busy with a career and raising a family. I never joined a veterans' group and didn't think about the war very much. It had been a very unpleasant subject for almost everyone at the time, and I was practiced in avoiding it as a topic of conversation.

Then in the spring of 2013, two events occurred that changed my outlook on the pictures. Arlene Addison, a friend and local high-school teacher who had heard of my experiences, asked me to make a presentation to her advanced English classes. She had developed a classroom project based on war and literature. Students read books such as *Red Badge of Courage* and *All Quiet on the Western Front* that described the Civil War, the two World Wars, Korea, Vietnam, etc. I edited my slides down to a forty-five-minute presentation and shared them with the students. They were respectful and mature in the question-and-answer session that followed. I didn't think the presentation had much effect on them, but three days later Arlene handed me a folder containing sixty handwritten letters. Each student had composed a summary of their thoughts on the war and their impressions of my experience. They thanked me for taking the time to share it with them and also thanked me for my service. These were teenagers, who were born long after the war had ended. I was deeply moved by their letters.

A few weeks later, I was chatting with a small group from my sailing club at a bar in the Berkeley marina when someone mentioned a new book about the Vietnam War. I made a comment about the subject, and we discovered that three of us were army veterans of that era. Alan Weller had served with a helicopter pilot training unit in the south, and Tom Loughran had served at the Presidio in San Francisco. Alan asked me if I had any pictures from my tour. When I mentioned that I recently had given a presentation at a local high school, he said that he would love to see the pictures and could arrange a special evening event for military veterans and local historians.

We agreed on a date in August, which gave me three months to scan all of the images and then edit them down to a ninety-minute presentation. As I began the process, I was amazed when I realized that I had more than four thousand pictures. Roughly half were color slides and the rest were black-and-white photos. The total number surprised me because the pictures had all been taken in the predigital era, when you only shot twenty-four or thirty-six pictures on a roll and then had to pay for developing and printing in order to see what you had captured in the camera.

In August a group of about twenty-five people attended the presentation in Berkeley. I began by saying that it was a day that I had never expected. If someone had told me years earlier that I would be making a presentation on the Vietnam War to a group in Berkeley, I would have said they were crazy. Berkeley was one of the centers of the most vigorous antiwar protests during the entire conflict. Yet, on this day, there was a rapt audience who listened carefully and contributed their personal observations and experiences on the topic. When I finished, someone asked when the book was coming out. I had not seriously considered writing a book before this, but I responded with an off-the-cuff comment that it was possible. If I wrote a ten-word caption for each picture, I would have forty thousand words that could be a good start on a book. The next week I sat down and started to organize my thoughts. This book is the result.

# INDEX

## A

AFVN (Armed Forces Vietnam Radio/TV) · 12, 127, 128
AK-47 · 24, 71
APC (armored personnel carrier) · 54, 165
Apollo 7 · 106
Apollo 8 · 154
Army Commendation Medal · 121
ARVN (Army of Republic of Vietnam) · 25, 148, 196, 213, 224

## B

Bamboo poisoning · 30
Bien Hoa · 4, 182
Big Red One, (1st Infantry Division) · 5, 26, 146
Bishop, Joey · 132
Brighton Beach, Brooklyn · 35
Bronze Star · 121
Bruce · 167, 175, 227, 238, 263
Bubblegum machine · 132, 160, 167
Buddhist · 206, 248
Bulldogs, 129th AHC · 165, 223

## C

C-4 Explosive · 23, 29, 56, 101, 192, 211
Camp LBJ · 52, 73
Caribou · 244
Cat Lai · 200
Chaplain · 29, 80
Chieu Hoi · 226
Chinook helicopter · 77, 112, 124, 135
CIB (Combat Infantryman Badge) · 112, 121

Gregorian chant · 62

---

### H

Hedren, Tippi · 132
Hootch · 13, 23, 28, 36, 74, 137, 220, 240
Hueys · 16, 23, 42, 66, 224

---

### J

Johnson, Lyndon · 52, 112, 129, 163
JP-4 · 18

---

### K

Kit Carson Scout · 113
Klick · 65, 107, 185
Ky, vice president, South Vietnam · 34

---

### L

Lambretta · 54, 67, 138, 223, 236
Leeches · 39
Loan, Police Chief · 34
LOH (light observation helicopter) · 84
Long Binh · 4, 52, 182, 263
L-shaped ambush · 95, 107, 201
LST · 221

---

### M

M-1 carbine · 71, 99
M-113-ACAV · 237

## N

## O

## P

Made in the USA
San Bernardino, CA
14 May 2015